WOMEN'S
2025

FOOTBALL
LEGENDS

PUBLISHED FOR THE USA IN 2024 BY WELBECK CHILDREN'S BOOKS
An imprint of Hachette Children's Group
Part of Hodder & Stoughton Limited
Carmelite House, 50 Victoria Embankment, London, EC4Y 0DZ
An Hachette UK Company
www.hachette.co.uk
www.hachettechildrens.co.uk

All statistical data and player heat maps provided by Opta, under license from Stats Perform.

DISCLAIMER

10 9 8 7 6 5 4 3 2 1
ISBN 978 1 8045 3732 9

Printed and bound in Dubai
Author: Kevin Pettman
Senior Commissioning Editor: Suhel Ahmed
Design Manager: Matt Drew
Picture research: Paul Langan
Production: Melanie Robertson

PICTURE CREDITS

The publishers would like to thank the following sources for their kind permission to reproduce the pictures in this book.

GETTY IMAGES: Eric Alonso 8; ANP 60, 79; Marc Atkins 108B; Naomi Baker/The FA 78; Ira L. Black/Corbis 106T, 110T; Bagu Blanco/Pressinphoto/Icon Sport 40; Jose Breton/Pics Action/NurPhoto 16, 38, 59, 77; Rico Brouwer/Soccrates 72; Henry Browne/The FA 111B; Alex Burstow/Arsenal FC 14, 22, 46; Alex Caparros 63; Steph Chambers 108T; Jenny Chuang/ISI Photos 19, 98; Seb Daly/Sportsfile 17; Kelly Defina 109T; Graham Denholm 102; Elianton/Mondadori Portfolio 51; Eurasia Sport Images 39; Jacques Feeney/Offside 44, 52; Baptiste Fernandez/Icon Sport 18, 106B; Franck Fife/AFP 35, 85; Nigel French/Sportsphoto/Allstar 15; Scott Gardiner 109B; Gaspafotos/MB Media 99; Edith Geuppert/GES Sportfoto 76; Rich Graessle/Icon Sportswire 101; Alex Grimm 30, 53; Oliver Hardt 64, 74, 93, 111T; Jose Hernandez/Anadolu Agency 69; Mike Hewitt 47; Christian Hofer/UEFA 61; Harry How 42; Saeed Khan/AFP 33; Christof Koepsel 49; Harriet Lander/Chelsea FC 36; Harriet Lander/The FA 56; Roy Lazet/Soccrates 55; Chris Lee/Chelsea FC 97; Christian Liewig/Corbis 27; Warren Little 87; Alex Livesey 95; Katharine Lotze 82; Marcio Machado/Eurasia Sport Images 21; Ian MacNicol 57; Ian MacNicol/The FA 90; Carmen Mandato 88; Steven Markham/Icon Sportswire 86; Matt McNulty 107T; Pablo Morano/MB Media 23; C. Morgan Engel 105; Jonathan Moscrop 92; Doug Murray/Icon Sportswire 96; Alex Pantling/UEFA 65; Ulrik Pedersen/DeFodi Images 83; Richard Pelham/The FA 13, 31; Ryan Pierse 9; Daniel Pockett 28; Daniela Porcelli/Eurasia Sport Images 103; Joe Prior/Visionhaus 10, 54, 67, 71; Manuel Queimadelos/Quality Sport Images 11, 89; David Ramirez/Quality Sport Images 25; David Ramos 5, 34, 45, 70; Sandra Ruhaut/Icon Sport 91; Will Russell 12; Pedro Salado 26, 107B; Pedro Salado/Quality Sport Images 29; Fran Santiago/The FA 20; Richard Sellers/Sportsphoto/Allstar 48, 75; Justin Setterfield 24; Brad Smith/ISI Photos/USSF 80; Howard Smith/ISI Photos 73; Diego Souto 50, 94; Janelle St Pierre 62, 68; Darrian Traynor 66; Kenzo Tribouillard/AFP 100; Omar Vega 37, 43; Visionhaus 41, 81; Sebastian Widmann 110B; Evan Yu 7
OTHER: Vecteezy.com, Shutterstock/Design_Lands, Shutterstock/Shiraufa's art

Every effort has been made to acknowledge correctly and contact the source and/or copyright holder of each picture; any unintentional errors or omissions will be corrected in future editions of this book.

All data correct up to May 2024

WOMEN'S 2025
FOOTBALL LEGENDS

STATS • PROFILES • TOP PLAYERS

WELBECK
CHILDREN'S BOOKS

CONTENTS

HOW TO USE THE BOOK................5

DEFENDERS................6
Ona Batlle................8
Millie Bright................9
Lucy Bronze................10
Olga Carmona................11
Elllie Carpenter................12
Jess Carter................13
Steph Catley................14
Niamh Charles................15
Magdalena Eriksson................16
Vanessa Gilles................17
Naomi Girma................18
Alex Greenwood................19
Kathrin Hendrich................20
Amanda Ilestedt................21
Sakina Karchaoui................22
Ashley Lawrence................23
Mapi León................24
Katie McCabe................25
Irene Paredes................26
Wendie Renard................27
Rebekah Stott................28
Marta Torrejón................29
Glódís Viggósdóttir................30
Leah Williamson................31

MIDFIELDERS................32
Aitana Bonmatí................34
Delphine Cascarino................35
Erin Cuthbert................36
Debinha................37
Crystal Dunn................38
Grace Geyoro................39
Patri Guijarro................40
Lauren Hemp................41
Lindsey Horan................42

Rose Lavelle................43
Kim Little................44
Vicky López................45
Frida Maanum................46
Lieke Martens................47
Hinara Miyazawa................48
Lena Oberdorf................49
Clàudia Pina................50
Alexia Putellas................51
Guro Reiten................52
Georgia Stanway................53
Ella Toone................54
Daniëlle van de Donk................55
Keira Walsh................56
Caroline Weir................57

FORWARDS................58
Klara Bühl................60
Kadidiatou Diani................61
Caitlin Foord................62
Caroline Graham Hansen................63
Pernille Harder................64
Ada Hegerberg................65
Michelle Heyman................66
Lauren James................67
Sam Kerr................68
Racheal Kundananji................69
Eugénie Le Sommer................70
Beth Mead................71
Vivianne Miedema................72
Alex Morgan................73
Ewa Pajor................74
Salma Paralluelo................75
Alexandra Popp................76
Fridolina Rolfö................77
Alessia Russo................78
Lea Schüller................79
Jaedyn Shaw................80

Khadija Shaw................81
Sophia Smith................82
Hannah Wilkinson................83

GOALKEEPERS................84
Mackenzie Arnold................86
Ann-Katrin Berger................87
Jane Campbell................88
Catalina Coll................89
Mary Earps................90
Christiane Endler................91
Merle Frohms................92
Maria Luisa Grohs................93
Emma Holmgren................94
Kiara Keating................95
Casey Murphy................96
Zećira Mušović................97
Alyssa Naeher................98
Chiamaka Nnadozie................99
Sandra Paños................100
Kailen Sheridan................101
Lydia Williams................102
Manuela Zinsberger................103

MANAGERS................104
Juan Carlos Amorós................106
Sonia Bompastor................
Jonas Eidevall................107
Jonatan Giráldez................
Laura Harvey................108
Emma Hayes................
Jeff Hopkins................109
Ante Juric................
Casey Stoney................110
Alexander Straus................
Tommy Stroot................111
Gareth Taylor................

HOW TO USE THIS BOOK

Welcome to *Football Legends 2025 (Women)* — packed with the latest performance stats of today's top players and coaches in the women's game! We have selected more than 100 stars from the world's best leagues including the National Women's Soccer League (NWSL) in the USA, the Women's Super League (WSL) in England, Australia's A-League, as well as the elite women's leagues in Spain, France and Germany. The players and coaches have spent at least the past two years of their careers operating in these top leagues. With all the key stats at your fingertips, you can use this book to anaylse their career performances and determine who are currently the finest defenders, midfielders, forwards, goalkeepers and managers in the world.

The types of stats featured for each position vary, because each position performs a specific role on the field. For example, a defender's main job is to stop the opposition from scoring, so the stats focus mainly on this part of that player's game. Likewise, a striker's tackling is not as relevant as their goal or assists tally. What you will find for all the players is their heat map which shows the areas of the field they focus their play in or, with goalkeepers, whether their strengths lie in the six-yard box or playing as sweeper keepers, who are comfortable all around the penalty area.

The stats relate to a player's performances over the past two seasons (2022/23 and 2023/24), as members of teams belonging to one of the top leagues. The only exception lies with NWSL players, whose stats cover the the 2022 and 2023 seasons, plus the first 10 matches of the 2024 season. The figures have been collected from domestic league and European match appearances (the latter not applying to players in NWSL, of course) and exclude data from domestic cup, super cups or international games.

DEFENDERS

In modern elite-level football, a defender is much more than a player purely there to stop the opposition scoring. While that remains the priority, defenders also help build attacks by calmly bringing the ball out from the back or making a long-range pass. Defensive positions include centre-backs, full-backs and wing-backs. There can be two or three centre-backs in a team and they are usually tall with the power to tackle and good height to head the ball away. Full-backs and wing-backs operate in wide areas and they must have the speed, skill and energy to defend their box and make penetrating forward runs.

WHAT DO THESE STATS MEAN?

 75%

AERIAL DUELS WON
This is the percentage of headers a defender has won in her own penalty area to interrupt an opposition attack.

INTERCEPTIONS
The number of times a defender has successfully stopped an attack without needing to make a tackle.

BLOCKS
A shot that is intercepted by a defender – preventing her keeper from having to make a save.

PASS ACCURACY
Pass accuracy indicates, as a percentage, the player's ability to complete a pass to a team-mate.

CLEARANCES
An attack successfully foiled, either by kicking or heading the ball away from danger.

TACKLES
The number of times a defender has challenged and dispossessed the opposition without committing a foul.

Did you **know?**

Unlike many teams in the NWSL, San Diego Wave tend not to dominate games in wide areas or press high. Instead, the team relies on compact defending with players such as Naomi Girma (right) often making a key pass to begin a counterattack.

22

ONA BATLLE

Ona Batlle was a Barcelona youth player before developing her attacking and defensive skills at Levante and Manchester United. The right-back re-joined Barca in 2023 and her eye-catching runs and strong tackling have since become a standout feature of her game.

DATE OF BIRTH	10/06/1999
POSITION	RIGHT-BACK
HEIGHT	1.65 M
PRO DEBUT	2014
PREFERRED FOOT	RIGHT

APPEARANCES
50

BLOCKS
10

INTERCEPTIONS
61

AERIAL DUELS WON
53.7%

PASS COMPLETION
86.5%

PENALTIES SCORED
0

GOALS
4

PASSES
2736

CLEARANCES
37

TACKLES
127

MAJOR CLUB HONOURS
⚽ UEFA Women's Champions League: 2024 ⚽ Liga F: 2024 ⚽ Copa de la Reina: 2017, 2024 ⚽ Women's FA Cup: Runner-up 2023 (Manchester United)

INTERNATIONAL HONOURS
⚽ FIFA Women's World Cup: 2023
⚽ UEFA Women's Nations League: 2024

ACTIVITY AREAS

MILLIE BRIGHT

After spending her early career in midfield, Millie Bright became a centre-back where her accurate passing and clever movement combined with her powerful heading and interceptions make her immense. She is a brilliant leader on the pitch too.

 **NATIONALITY**
English

CURRENT CLUB
Chelsea

 4

DATE OF BIRTH	21/08/1993
POSITION	CENTRAL
HEIGHT	1.75 M
PRO DEBUT	2009
PREFERRED FOOT	RIGHT

BLOCKS
15

APPEARANCES
31

INTERCEPTIONS
43

AERIAL DUELS WON
71.1%

PENALTIES SCORED
0

PASS COMPLETION
84.1%

GOALS
3

PASSES
2175

CLEARANCES
88

TACKLES
34

MAJOR CLUB HONOURS
- Women's Super League: 2015, 2018, 2020, 2021, 2022, 2023
- UEFA Women's Champions League: runner-up 2021
- Women's FA Cup: 2015, 2018, 2021, 2022, 2023, 2024
- Women's FA League Cup: 2020, 2021

INTERNATIONAL HONOURS
- UEFA Women's Championship: 2022
- FIFA Women's World Cup: runner-up 2023

ACTIVITY AREAS

9

15

NATIONALITY
English

CURRENT CLUB
Barcelona

LUCY BRONZE

For more than a decade now, Lucy Bronze has been among the best full-backs in world football. She's known for her energy, clean tackling and bursting right-wing raids. What's more, she has a knack for scoring headers from free-kicks and corners.

DATE OF BIRTH	28/10/1991
POSITION	RIGHT-BACK
HEIGHT	1.72 M
PRO DEBUT	2007
PREFERRED FOOT	RIGHT

BLOCKS
9

APPEARANCES
59

INTERCEPTIONS
86

AERIAL DUELS WON
66.2%

PASS COMPLETION
84%

PENALTIES SCORED
0

GOALS
5

PASSES
3,124

CLEARANCES
46

TACKLES
103

MAJOR CLUB HONOURS

⚽ Liga F: 2023, 2024 ⚽ UEFA Women's Champions League: 2023, 2018*, 2019*, 2020* (*Lyon), 2024 ⚽ Division 1 Féminine: 2018, 2019, 2020 (all Lyon) ⚽ Women's Super League: 2013, 2014* (*Liverpool), 2016 (Manchester City) ⚽ Coupe de France Féminine: 2019, 2020 (all Lyon)

INTERNATIONAL HONOURS

⚽ UEFA Women's Championship: 2022
⚽ FIFA Women's World Cup: runner-up 2023
⚽ Women's Finalissima: 2023

ACTIVITY AREAS

OLGA CARMONA

Scoring the winning goals in both the semi-final and final of the 2023 FIFA World Cup catapulted Olga Carmona to global stardom. A stylish defender, when Carmona dispossesses an opponent, expect to see her power forward with the ball and test the goalkeeper or expertly pick out a team-mate.

NATIONALITY
Spanish

CURRENT CLUB
Real Madrid

7

DATE OF BIRTH	06/12/2000
POSITION	LEFT-BACK
HEIGHT	1.60 M
PRO DEBUT	2017
PREFERRED FOOT	LEFT

APPEARANCES
62

INTERCEPTIONS
76

BLOCKS
6

AERIAL DUELS WON
41.5%

PASS COMPLETION
78.5%

GOALS
11

PENALTIES SCORED
7

PASSES
2,394

CLEARANCES
46

TACKLES
122

MAJOR CLUB HONOURS
⚽ None to date

INTERNATIONAL HONOURS
⚽ FIFA Women's World Cup: 2023
⚽ UEFA Women's Nations League: 2024

ACTIVITY AREAS

12

NATIONALITY
Australian

CURRENT CLUB
Lyon

ELLIE CARPENTER

Ever reliable at the back, Ellie Carpenter can shut down attacks in her box with great speed. She's also adept at making overlapping runs and cleverly pulling opponents out of position, which makes her a menace at the attacking end of the pitch.

DATE OF BIRTH	28/04/2000
POSITION	RIGHT-BACK
HEIGHT	1.64 M
PRO DEBUT	2015
PREFERRED FOOT	RIGHT

APPEARANCES
36

INTERCEPTIONS
27

BLOCKS
4

PENALTIES SCORED
0

AERIAL DUELS WON
28%

PASS COMPLETION
83.5%

GOALS
0

PASSES
1,480

CLEARANCES
23

TACKLES
75

MAJOR CLUB HONOURS
⚽ Division 1 Féminine: 2022, 2023, 2024 ⚽ UEFA Women's Champions League: 2020, 2022, runner-up 2024 ⚽ Coupe de France Féminine: 2020, 2023 ⚽ A-League Premiership: 2020 (Melbourne City) ⚽ A-League Championship: 2020 (Melbourne City)

INTERNATIONAL HONOURS
⚽ None to date

ACTIVITY AREAS

JESS CARTER

Jess Carter's versatility means she can play across the defensive line and even in midfield. Robust in possession and with quick acceleration, she enjoys battles against tall strikers and speedy wingers, winning those clashes more often than not.

NATIONALITY
English

CURRENT CLUB
Chelsea

DATE OF BIRTH	27/10/1997
POSITION	CENTRAL
HEIGHT	1.65 M
PRO DEBUT	2013
PREFERRED FOOT	RIGHT

APPEARANCES
55

INTERCEPTIONS
53

BLOCKS
23

AERIAL DUELS WON
53.3%

PASS COMPLETION
85.9%

GOALS
2

PENALTIES SCORED
0

PASSES
2,856

CLEARANCES
155

TACKLES
110

MAJOR CLUB HONOURS
⚽ Women's Super League: 2020, 2021, 2022, 2023, 2024
⚽ UEFA Women's Champions League: runner-up 2021
⚽ Women's FA Cup: 2021, 2022, 2023
⚽ Women's FA League Cup: 2020, 2021

INTERNATIONAL HONOURS
⚽ UEFA Women's Championship: 2022
⚽ FIFA Women's World Cup: runner-up 2023
⚽ Women's Finalissima: 2023

ACTIVITY AREAS

13

12

NATIONALITY
Australian

CURRENT CLUB
Arsenal

STEPH CATLEY

The Australian Steph Catley is dynamic down the left-wing. She will routinely collect the ball in tight defensive positions and coolly play out or make a superb cross-field pass. Her delivery from set pieces regularly sets up scoring chances.

DATE OF BIRTH	26/01/1994
POSITION	LEFT-BACK
HEIGHT	1.71 M
PRO DEBUT	2009
PREFERRED FOOT	LEFT

BLOCKS
10

APPEARANCES
47

INTERCEPTIONS
22

AERIAL DUELS WON
47.4%

PENALTIES SCORED
0

GOALS
2

PASS COMPLETION
86.3%

PASSES
1,970

CLEARANCES
56

TACKLES
52

MAJOR CLUB HONOURS
⚽ A-League Championship: 2014 (Melbourne Victory), 2016, 2017, 2018, 2020 (all Melbourne City) ⚽ A-League Premiership: 2016, 2020 (Melbourne City) ⚽ Women's FA Cup: 2023 ⚽ Women's FA League Cup: 2023, 2024

INTERNATIONAL HONOURS
⚽ None to date

ACTIVITY AREAS

HEAT.R?

NIAMH CHARLES

Disciplined at the back and with strong leadership qualities, Niamh Charles is a bedrock in defence. Able to play on both flanks, she is known for passing and crossing well with either foot, darting inside or even sprinting down the touchline to set up attacks.

NATIONALITY
English

CURRENT CLUB
Chelsea

21

DATE OF BIRTH	21/06/1999
POSITION	FULL-BACK
HEIGHT	1.72 M
PRO DEBUT	2016
PREFERRED FOOT	RIGHT

APPEARANCES
62

INTERCEPTIONS
64

BLOCKS
9

AERIAL DUELS WON
66.4%

PASS COMPLETION
79.2%

GOALS
7

PENALTIES SCORED
0

TACKLES
139

PASSES
2,734

CLEARANCES
71

MAJOR CLUB HONOURS
⚽ Women's Super League: 2021, 2022, 2023, 2024
⚽ UEFA Women's Champions League: Runner-up 2021
⚽ Women's FA Cup: 2021, 2022, 2023
⚽ Women's FA League Cup: 2021

INTERNATIONAL HONOURS
⚽ FIFA Women's World Cup: runner-up 2023
⚽ Women's Finalissima: 2023

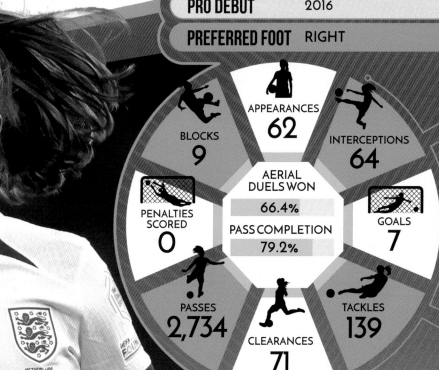

ACTIVITY AREAS

5

NATIONALITY
Swedish

CURRENT CLUB
Bayern Munich

MAGDALENA ERIKSSON

Somehow Magdalena Eriksson improves season after season to add to her reputation as an elite centre-back. She is calm in possession, strong in the air and able to ping laser-guided passes that break opposition defences.

DATE OF BIRTH	08/09/1993
POSITION	CENTRAL
HEIGHT	1.73 M
PRO DEBUT	2011
PREFERRED FOOT	LEFT

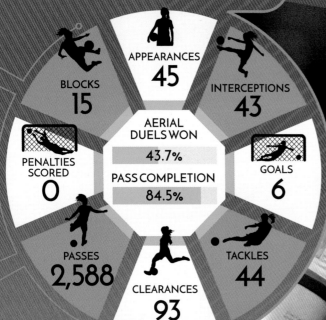

BLOCKS
15

APPEARANCES
45

INTERCEPTIONS
43

PENALTIES SCORED
0

AERIAL DUELS WON
43.7%

PASS COMPLETION
84.5%

GOALS
6

PASSES
2,588

CLEARANCES
93

TACKLES
44

MAJOR CLUB HONOURS
⚽ Frauen-Bundesliga: 2024 ⚽ Women's Super League: 2018, 2020, 2021, 2022, 2023 (all Chelsea) ⚽ Women's FA Cup: 2018, 2021, 2022, 2023 (all Chelsea) ⚽ UEFA Women's Champions League: Runner-up 2021 (Chelsea)

INTERNATIONAL HONOURS
⚽ FIFA Women's World Cup: third place 2019, third place 2023 ⚽ Olympic Games: runner-up 2016, 2020 (2021)

ACTIVITY AREAS

VANESSA GILLES

Winning one-on-ones, outjumping strikers and knowing exactly when to slide tackle are some of Vanessa Gilles' key skills. Her upper-body strength and fearless approach to defending gives her club and country a formidable barrier.

NATIONALITY
Canadian

CURRENT CLUB
Lyon (on loan)

21

DATE OF BIRTH	11/03/1996
POSITION	CENTRAL
HEIGHT	1.74 M
PRO DEBUT	2017
PREFERRED FOOT	RIGHT

APPEARANCES
55

BLOCKS
28

INTERCEPTIONS
81

AERIAL DUELS WON
70.7%

PENALTIES SCORED
0

GOALS
11

PASS COMPLETION
86.4%

PASSES
2,768

CLEARANCES
186

TACKLES
81

MAJOR CLUB HONOURS
- Division 1 Féminine: 2023, 2024
- Coupe de France Féminine: 2023
- UEFA Women's Champions League: runner-up 2024

INTERNATIONAL HONOURS
- Olympic Games: 2020 (2021)

ACTIVITY AREAS

4

NATIONALITY
American

CURRENT CLUB
San Diego Wave

NAOMI GIRMA

Naomi Girma has made a rapid rise in world football. She reads the game brilliantly, knowing when to step in and make a challenge, which makes her tough to beat on the ground and in the air. Her consistent performances saw her scoop the NWSL Defender of the Year prize two seasons in a row.

DATE OF BIRTH	14/06/2000
POSITION	CENTRAL
HEIGHT	1.68 M
PRO DEBUT	2022
PREFERRED FOOT	RIGHT

BLOCKS
41

APPEARANCES
47

INTERCEPTIONS
44

PENALTIES SCORED
0

AERIAL DUELS WON
50.6%

PASS COMPLETION
87.1%

GOALS
0

PASSES
2,599

CLEARANCES
224

TACKLES
72

MAJOR CLUB HONOURS
⚽ NWSL Shield: 2023

INTERNATIONAL HONOURS
⚽ CONCACAF Women's Gold Cup: 2024
⚽ CONCACAF Women's Championship: 2022

ACTIVITY AREAS

ALEX GREENWOOD

Playing left-back or her preferred centre-back role, Alex Greenwood is a quick and powerful presence who protects her goal at all costs. She has a quick-thinking footy brain and is difficult to knock off the ball. Her free-kick technique gives her team another edge in attack.

NATIONALITY
English

CURRENT CLUB
Manchester City

5

DATE OF BIRTH	07/09/1993
POSITION	CENTRAL
HEIGHT	1.67 M
PRO DEBUT	2010
PREFERRED FOOT	LEFT

APPEARANCES
41

BLOCKS
28

INTERCEPTIONS
65

AERIAL DUELS WON
48.7%

PASS COMPLETION
87.6%

PENALTIES SCORED
0

GOALS
1

PASSES
3,609

CLEARANCES
100

TACKLES
53

MAJOR CLUB HONOURS
⚽ Division 1 Féminine: 2020 (Lyon) ⚽ UEFA Women's Champions League: 2020 (Lyon) ⚽ Coupe de France Féminine: 2020 (Lyon) ⚽ Women's FA Cup: 2020 ⚽ Women's FA League Cup: 2022

INTERNATIONAL HONOURS
⚽ UEFA Women's Championship: 2022
⚽ FIFA Women's World Cup: runner-up 2023
⚽ Women's Finalissima: 2023

ACTIVITY AREAS

4

NATIONALITY
German

CURRENT CLUB
VfL Wolfsburg

KATHRIN HENDRICH

Kathrin Hendrich offers defensive and attacking qualities for club and country. A ball-playing centre-back, she often breaks forward and releases key passes or drifts wide to whip crosses into the box. A fan favourite for sure.

DATE OF BIRTH	06/04/1992
POSITION	CENTRAL
HEIGHT	1.74 M
PRO DEBUT	2008
PREFERRED FOOT	RIGHT

BLOCKS
12

APPEARANCES
52

INTERCEPTIONS
48

PENALTIES SCORED
0

AERIAL DUELS WON
46.3%

PASS COMPLETION
88.9%

GOALS
0

PASSES
3,212

CLEARANCES
72

TACKLES
113

MAJOR CLUB HONOURS
- ⚽ Frauen-Bundesliga: 2022
- ⚽ UEFA Women's Champions League: 2015 (Frankfurt)
- ⚽ DFB-Pokal Frauen: 2021, 2022, 2023

INTERNATIONAL HONOURS
- ⚽ Olympic Games: 2016
- ⚽ UEFA Women's Championship: runner-up 2022

ACTIVITY AREAS

AMANDA ILESTEDT

Amanda Ilestedt is so difficult to beat in the air, using her height, power and impressive technique to win headers in both penalty boxes. She is hard to dispossess with the ball at her feet and makes difficult passes look simple.

NATIONALITY
Swedish

CURRENT CLUB
Arsenal

28

DATE OF BIRTH	17/01/1993
POSITION	CENTRAL
HEIGHT	1.78 M
PRO DEBUT	2008
PREFERRED FOOT	RIGHT

APPEARANCES
32

BLOCKS
18

INTERCEPTIONS
39

AERIAL DUELS WON
56.3%

PENALTIES SCORED
0

PASS COMPLETION
86.2%

GOALS
1

PASSES
1,955

CLEARANCES
72

TACKLES
38

MAJOR CLUB HONOURS
- ⚽ Frauen-Bundesliga: 2021 (Bayern Munich)
- ⚽ Coupe de France Féminine: 2022 (PSG)
- ⚽ Damallsvenskan: 2010, 2011, 2013, 2014 (all FC Rosengard)

INTERNATIONAL HONOURS
- ⚽ Olympic Games: runner-up 2016
- ⚽ FIFA Women's World Cup: third place 2019, third place 2023

ACTIVITY AREAS

7

NATIONALITY
French

CURRENT CLUB
Paris Saint-Germain

SAKINA KARCHAOUI

A defender who takes pride in keeping clean sheets, Sakina Karchaoui plays like a winger carrying a goal scoring threat. Her wide runs stretch the opposition and she is then able to deliver the ball to a team-mate in a prime spot inside the box.

DATE OF BIRTH	26/01/1996
POSITION	LEFT-BACK
HEIGHT	1.60 M
PRO DEBUT	2012
PREFERRED FOOT	LEFT

BLOCKS
7

APPEARANCES
52

INTERCEPTIONS
85

PENALTIES SCORED
1

AERIAL DUELS WON
55%

PASS COMPLETION
82.8%

GOALS
3

PASSES
3,288

CLEARANCES
42

TACKLES
73

MAJOR CLUB HONOURS
⚽ Coupe de France: 2022, 2024
⚽ UEFA Women's Champions League: 2020 (Lyon)

INTERNATIONAL HONOURS
⚽ None to date

ACTIVITY AREAS

ASHLEY LAWRENCE

Ashley Lawrence is such a valuable team player because she can play both at left- and right-back. While drilled at keeping danger away from her own box, the defender can also inject creativity and flair into the team with her speedy runs and accurate crosses.

CURRENT CLUB
Chelsea

26

DATE OF BIRTH	11/06/1995
POSITION	RIGHT/LEFT
HEIGHT	1.68 M
PRO DEBUT	2013
PREFERRED FOOT	RIGHT

BLOCKS
10

APPEARANCES
53

INTERCEPTIONS
29

PENALTIES SCORED
0

AERIAL DUELS WON
29.7%

PASS COMPLETION
82.4%

GOALS
1

PASSES
2,220

CLEARANCES
30

TACKLES
84

MAJOR CLUB HONOURS
⚽ Women's Super League: 2024 ⚽ Division 1 Féminine: 2021 (PSG) ⚽ Coupe de France: 2018, 2022 (all PSG) ⚽ UEFA Women's Champions League: Runner-up 2017 (PSG)

INTERNATIONAL HONOURS
⚽ Olympic Games: 2020 (2021)

ACTIVITY AREAS

NATIONALITY
Spanish

CURRENT CLUB
Barcelona

MAPI LEÓN

A tough centre-back who makes hard but fair challenges with her head and feet, Mapi León is a leader in defence. Playing a high press, she has the confidence to control her line and spring attacks with a telling pass from her cultured left foot.

DATE OF BIRTH	13/06/1995
POSITION	CENTRAL
HEIGHT	1.70 M
PRO DEBUT	2009
PREFERRED FOOT	LEFT

BLOCKS
7

APPEARANCES
46

INTERCEPTIONS
56

AERIAL DUELS WON
51.5%

PASS COMPLETION
90.1%

PENALTIES SCORED
0

GOALS
6

PASSES
3,892

CLEARANCES
37

TACKLES
51

MAJOR CLUB HONOURS
⚽ Liga F: 2017 (Atlético Madrid) 2020, 2021, 2022, 2023, 2024 ⚽ UEFA Women's Champions League: 2021, 2023, 2024 ⚽ Copa de la Reina: 2016 (Atlético Madrid), 2018, 2020, 2021, 2022, 2024

INTERNATIONAL HONOURS
⚽ None to date

ACTIVITY AREAS

KATIE MCCABE

While a stalwart in defence, Katie McCabe is blessed with the technique and determination to cover so much of the pitch. Her forward runs are perfectly timed and there are not many players who hit left-footed shots quite as sweetly.

NATIONALITY
Republic of Ireland

CURRENT CLUB
Arsenal

15

DATE OF BIRTH	21/09/1995
POSITION	LEFT BACK
HEIGHT	1.68 M
PRO DEBUT	2011
PREFERRED FOOT	LEFT

BLOCKS
5

APPEARANCES
52

INTERCEPTIONS
36

PENALTIES SCORED
0

AERIAL DUELS WON
23.3%

PASS COMPLETION
81.1%

GOALS
6

PASSES
2,054

CLEARANCES
41

TACKLES
81

MAJOR CLUB HONOURS
- Women's Super League: 2019
- Women's FA Cup: 2016
- Women's FA League Cup: 2018, 2023, 2024

INTERNATIONAL HONOURS
- None to date

ACTIVITY AREAS

NATIONALITY
Spanish

CURRENT CLUB
Barcelona

IRENE PAREDES

Few players are better than Irene Paredes when it comes to making a well-timed interception and using flair and vision to deliver the ball to a team-mate in an attacking position. The dominant centre-back uses her physique to marshall her defensive zone and connect with corners at the other end.

DATE OF BIRTH	04/07/1991
POSITION	CENTRAL
HEIGHT	1.78 M
PRO DEBUT	2008
PREFERRED FOOT	RIGHT

BLOCKS
19

APPEARANCES
60

INTERCEPTIONS
80

AERIAL DUELS WON
67.1%

PASS COMPLETION
90.6%

PENALTIES SCORED
0

GOALS
4

PASSES
4,199

CLEARANCES
78

TACKLES
62

MAJOR CLUB HONOURS
⚽ Liga F: 2016 (Athletic Bilbao), 2022, 2023, 2024 ⚽
UEFA Women's Champions League: 2023, 2024 ⚽ Copa de
la Reina: 2022, 2024 ⚽ Division 1 Féminine: 2018 (PSG)
⚽ Coupe de France Féminine: 2018 (PSG)

INTERNATIONAL HONOURS
⚽ FIFA Women's World Cup: 2023
⚽ UEFA Women's Nations League: 2024

ACTIVITY AREAS

WENDIE RENARD

The towering Wendie Renard has a trophy cabinet that befits her status as a world-class player. She uses her tall frame and athletic skills to defend her goal and moves like a sprinter when she has to track back or give chase. For more than a decade she has been a matchwinner for both club and country.

NATIONALITY
French

CURRENT CLUB
Lyon

3

DATE OF BIRTH	20/07/1990
POSITION	CENTRAL
HEIGHT	1.87 M
PRO DEBUT	2006
PREFERRED FOOT	RIGHT

BLOCKS
8

APPEARANCES
48

INTERCEPTIONS
66

PENALTIES SCORED
3

AERIAL DUELS WON
82.7%

PASS COMPLETION
87.4%

GOALS
13

PASSES
2,824

CLEARANCES
96

TACKLES
49

MAJOR CLUB HONOURS
⚽ Division 1 Féminine: 2007, 2008, 2009, 2010, 2011, 2012, 2013, 2014, 2015, 2016, 2017, 2018, 2019, 2020, 2022, 2023, 2024 ⚽ UEFA Champions League: 2011, 2012, 2016, 2017, 2018, 2019, 2020, 2022, runner-up, 2024 ⚽ Coupe de France: 2008, 2012–2017, 2019, 2020, 2023

INTERNATIONAL HONOURS
⚽ None to date

ACTIVITY AREAS

13

NATIONALITY
New Zealand

CURRENT CLUB
Melbourne City

REBEKAH STOTT

With more than a century of international and A-League (formerly W-League) appearances, Rebekah Stott always delivers influential displays. Superb at reading and breaking up play, she can follow that up with her top quality passing once the ball is at her feet.

DATE OF BIRTH	17/06/1993
POSITION	CENTRAL
HEIGHT	1.72 M
PRO DEBUT	2010
PREFERRED FOOT	RIGHT

APPEARANCES
27

BLOCKS
26

INTERCEPTIONS
61

AERIAL DUELS WON
34.6%

PASS COMPLETION
84.5%

PENALTIES SCORED
0

GOALS
1

PASSES
1,935

CLEARANCES
84

TACKLES
40

MAJOR CLUB HONOURS
⚽ A-League Championship: 2011 (Brisbane Roar), 2016, 2017, 2018, 2020, ⚽ A-League Premiership: 2016, 2020

INTERNATIONAL HONOURS
⚽ None to date

ACTIVITY AREAS

MARTA TORREJÓN

A Barcelona player since 2013, Marta Torrejón is a valued member because she can play across the defence. Whether heading balls clear at centre-back or attacking from full-back, her impact has driven Barça to domestic and European success in recent seasons.

NATIONALITY
Spanish

CURRENT CLUB
Barcelona

DATE OF BIRTH	27/02/1990
POSITION	CENTRAL
HEIGHT	1.71 M
PRO DEBUT	2004
PREFERRED FOOT	RIGHT

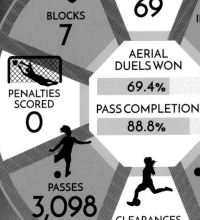

BLOCKS
7

APPEARANCES
69

INTERCEPTIONS
53

PENALTIES SCORED
0

AERIAL DUELS WON
69.4%

PASS COMPLETION
88.8%

GOALS
13

PASSES
3,098

CLEARANCES
36

TACKLES
43

MAJOR CLUB HONOURS
⚽ Liga F: 2006 (Espanyol), 2014, 2015, 2020, 2021, 2022, 2023, 2024 ⚽ UEFA Women's Champions League: 2021, 2023, 2024 ⚽ Copa de la Reina: 2006, 2009, 2010, 2012 (all Espanyol), 2014, 2017, 2018, 2020, 2021, 2022, 2024

INTERNATIONAL HONOURS
⚽ None to date

ACTIVITY AREAS

4

NATIONALITY
Icelandic

CURRENT CLUB
Bayern Munich

GLÓDÍS VIGGÓSDÓTTIR

Wearing the captain's armband at Bayern Munich and forming the lynchpin of their defence, Glódís Viggósdóttir consistently performs to a very high level. She combines her clever defending skills with a coolness when bringing the ball out from her half.

DATE OF BIRTH	27/06/1995
POSITION	CENTRAL
HEIGHT	1.73 M
PRO DEBUT	2009
PREFERRED FOOT	RIGHT

BLOCKS
50

APPEARANCES
57

INTERCEPTIONS
67

PENALTIES SCORED
0

AERIAL DUELS WON
65.4%

PASS COMPLETION
88.9%

GOALS
4

PASSES
4,698

CLEARANCES
220

TACKLES
62

MAJOR CLUB HONOURS
⚽ Frauen-Bundesliga: 2023, 2024
⚽ Damallsvenskan: 2019 (FC Rosengard)

INTERNATIONAL HONOURS
⚽ None to date

ACTIVITY AREAS

30

LEAH WILLIAMSON

Leah Williamson has an impressive footballing brain. She can sense danger and get into the best positions to deal with even the smartest forwards. What's more, with the athleticism to reach the ball first, she can build play intelligently from defence.

NATIONALITY
English

CURRENT CLUB
Arsenal

6

DATE OF BIRTH	29/06/1997
POSITION	CENTRAL
HEIGHT	1.70 M
PRO DEBUT	2014
PREFERRED FOOT	RIGHT

APPEARANCES
26

BLOCKS
10

INTERCEPTIONS
29

AERIAL DUELS WON
54.1%

PASS COMPLETION
83.6%

PENALTIES SCORED
0

GOALS
1

PASSES
1,783

CLEARANCES
28

TACKLES
28

MAJOR CLUB HONOURS
- ⚽ Women's Super League: 2019
- ⚽ Women's FA Cup: 2014, 2016
- ⚽ Women's FA League Cup: 2015, 2018, 2023, 2024

INTERNATIONAL HONOURS
- ⚽ UEFA Women's Championship: 2022
- ⚽ Women's Finalissima: 2023

ACTIVITY AREAS

MIDFIELDERS

Whether defensive, playmaker or operating just behind the forwards, midfielders are crucial to their team's success. A midfielder needs to be technically sound, a quick thinker and have the fitness to cover big distances during a game. Defensive midfielders protect their back line with strength and timely interceptions. Playmakers are more attack minded and have the job of creating scoring chances. Midfielders can even play close to the strikers in a role that's difficult for the opposition to track and pick up.

WHAT DO THE STATS MEAN?

ASSISTS
A pass, cross or header to a teammate who then scores counts as an assist. This stat also includes a deflected shot that is converted by a team-mate.

SHOTS
Any deliberate strike on goal counts as a shot. The strike does not have to be on target or force a save from the keeper.

CHANCES CREATED
Any pass that results in a shot at goal (whether or not the goal is scored) is regarded as a chance created.

TACKLES

This is the number of times the player has challenged and dispossessed the opposition without committing a foul.

DRIBBLES
This is the number of times the player has gone past an opponent while running with the ball.

75%

SUCCESSFUL PASSES
This shows, as a percentage, how successful the midfielder is at finding team-mates with passes.

Did you
know?

At the 2023 FIFA Women's World Cup, the top midfielders covered more than 77 km (48 miles) in total during their tournament appearances.

14

NATIONALITY
Spanish

CURRENT CLUB
Barcelona

AITANA BONMATÍ

With stacks of club and personal prizes, Aitana Bonmatí can score and create from even the slightest of chances. She has exquisite close control, is a dazzling dribbler and famed for delivering pinpoint crosses. She can be a real game changer in the big games.

DATE OF BIRTH	18/01/1998
POSITION	ATTACKING
HEIGHT	1.62 M
PRO DEBUT	2014
PREFERRED FOOT	RIGHT

APPEARANCES
69

ASSISTS
33

DRIBBLES
180

PASSES
3,525

SUCCESSFUL PASSES
87.5%

PENALTIES SCORED
0

GOALS
28

SHOTS
183

CHANCES CREATED
158

TACKLES
70

MAJOR CLUB HONOURS
⚽ Liga F: 2020, 2021, 2022, 2023, 2024
⚽ UEFA Women's Champions League: 2021, 2023, 2024
⚽ Copa de la Reina: 2017, 2018, 2020, 2021, 2022, 2024

INTERNATIONAL HONOURS
⚽ FIFA Women's World Cup: 2023
⚽ UEFA Women's Nations League: 2024

ACTIVITY AREAS

DELPHINE CASCARINO

NATIONALITY
French

CURRENT CLUB
Lyon

20

In an attacking right-sided role, few players can match the speed, skill and end product of Delphine Cascarino. She has the tricks and flicks to beat defenders and will find a team-mate with a bending cross or a slick through-pass. She is a very capable scorer as well.

DATE OF BIRTH	05/02/1997
POSITION	WINGER
HEIGHT	1.64 M
PRO DEBUT	2015
PREFERRED FOOT	RIGHT

APPEARANCES
36

ASSISTS
5

DRIBBLES
155

PENALTIES SCORED
0

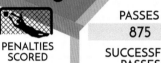
PASSES
875
SUCCESSFUL PASSES
75.1%

GOALS
9

SHOTS
63

CHANCES CREATED
61

TACKLES
40

MAJOR CLUB HONOURS
⚽ Division 1 Féminine: 2015, 2016, 2017, 2018, 2019, 2020, 2022, 2023, 2024 ⚽ UEFA Women's Champions League: 2016, 2017, 2018, 2019, 2020, runner-up 2024

INTERNATIONAL HONOURS
⚽ None to date

ACTIVITY AREAS

22

NATIONALITY
Scottish

CURRENT CLUB
Chelsea

ERIN CUTHBERT

Erin Cuthbert reached 50 goals for Chelsea in 2023. Her scoring rate in tandem with her incredible work rate in midfield means she is a big performer for the club. Versatile and committed in her tackling, the Scotland ace is a box-to-box menace for her opponents.

DATE OF BIRTH	19/07/1998
POSITION	CENTRAL
HEIGHT	1.59 M
PRO DEBUT	2013
PREFERRED FOOT	RIGHT

ASSISTS
5

APPEARANCES
38

DRIBBLES
48

PENALTIES SCORED
0

PASSES
1,655

SUCCESSFUL PASSES
83.6%

GOALS
9

SHOTS
83

CHANCES CREATED
40

TACKLES
94

MAJOR CLUB HONOURS
⚽ Women's Super League: 2017, 2018, 2020, 2021, 2022, 2023, 2024 ⚽ Women's FA Cup: 2018, 2021, 2022, 2023
⚽ UEFA Women's Champions League: runner-up 2021 ⚽ Women's FA League Cup: 2020, 2021

INTERNATIONAL HONOURS
⚽ None to date

ACTIVITY AREAS

DEBINHA

Opponents often double up on Debinha in a bid to contain the skills and forward bursts that make her shine. Whether operating as a central playmaker or drifting wide to unlock the defence in tight games, the Brazil star has that special X factor in her boots.

 **NATIONALITY**
Brazil

CURRENT CLUB
Kansas City Current

 99

DATE OF BIRTH	20/10/1991
POSITION	ATTACKING
HEIGHT	1.57 M
PRO DEBUT	2006
PREFERRED FOOT	RIGHT

APPEARANCES
43

ASSISTS
7

DRIBBLES
195

PENALTIES SCORED
3

PASSES
1,261
SUCCESSFUL PASSES
74.5%

GOALS
22

SHOTS
120

CHANCES CREATED
64

TACKLES
67

MAJOR CLUB HONOURS
- ⚽ NWSL Champions: 2018, 2019 (all North Carolina Courage)
- ⚽ NWSL Shield: 2017, 2018, 2019 (all North Carolina Courage)
- ⚽ NWSL Challenge Cup: 2022 (North Carolina Courage)

INTERNATIONAL HONOURS
- ⚽ Copa América Femenina: 2018, 2022

ACTIVITY AREAS

19

NATIONALITY
American

CURRENT CLUB
Manchester United

CRYSTAL DUNN

Capable of playing in midfield, attack and defensive roles, Crystal Dunn is a pivotal player who inspires top performances. Her pacey and explosive runs can tear defences apart. Alternatively, she can rein in her attacking game if a steady head is needed to grind out a result.

DATE OF BIRTH	03/07/1993
POSITION	CENTRAL
HEIGHT	1.57 M
PRO DEBUT	2014
PREFERRED FOOT	RIGHT

APPEARANCES
36

DRIBBLES
54

ASSISTS
2

PENALTIES SCORED
0

PASSES
814
SUCCESSFUL PASSES
79.2%

GOALS
6

SHOTS
50

CHANCES CREATED
40

TACKLES
56

MAJOR CLUB HONOURS
⚽ NWSL Championship: 2018, 2019 (all North Carolina Courage) 2022 (Portland Thorns) ⚽ NWSL Shield: 2018, 2019 (all North Carolina Shield), 2021 (Portland Thorns)

INTERNATIONAL HONOURS
⚽ FIFA Women's World Cup: 2019
⚽ CONCACAF Women's Championship: 2018
⚽ CONCACAF Women's Gold Cup: 2024

ACTIVITY AREAS

GRACE GEYORO

The Paris Saint-Germain captain keeps her team ticking between the boxes. Pouncing on mistakes and able to build counter attacks with one sweeping pass or surging run, Grace Geyoro revels as a gamechanger in midfield. She is an excellent header of the ball as well.

NATIONALITY
French

CURRENT CLUB
Paris Saint-Germain

8

DATE OF BIRTH	02/07/1997
POSITION	CENTRAL
HEIGHT	1.68 M
PRO DEBUT	2014
PREFERRED FOOT	RIGHT

APPEARANCES
59

ASSISTS
8

DRIBBLES
113

PENALTIES SCORED
3

PASSES
2,640
SUCCESSFUL PASSES
89.2%

GOALS
20

SHOTS
83

CHANCES CREATED
70

TACKLES
96

MAJOR CLUB HONOURS
⚽ Division 1 Féminine: 2021
⚽ Coupe de France Féminine: 2018, 2022, 2024
⚽ UEFA Women's Champions League: runner-up 2015, 2017

INTERNATIONAL HONOURS
⚽ None to date

ACTIVITY AREAS

12

PATRI GUIJARRO

Patri Guijarro sits deep in midfield, ready to break up attacks and set her team forward. Extremely tidy in challenges, she has a right foot that delivers perfect passes and her long-range shooting technique is among the very best.

DATE OF BIRTH	17/05/1998
POSITION	CENTRAL
HEIGHT	1.71 M
PRO DEBUT	2012
PREFERRED FOOT	RIGHT

APPEARANCES
69

DRIBBLES
66

ASSISTS
17

PASSES
5,125

SUCCESSFUL PASSES
86.8%

GOALS
15

PENALTIES SCORED
0

SHOTS
137

CHANCES CREATED
121

TACKLES
103

MAJOR CLUB HONOURS
⚽ Liga F: 2020, 2021, 2022, 2023, 2024
⚽ UEFA Women's Champions League: 2021, 2023, 2024
⚽ Copa de la Reina: 2017, 2018, 2020, 2021, 2024

INTERNATIONAL HONOURS
⚽ None to date

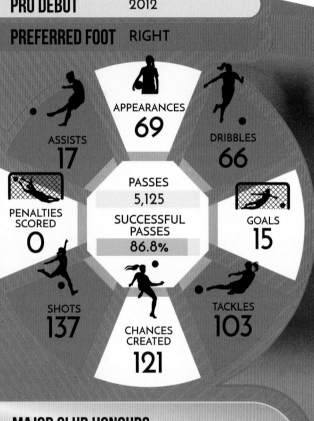

ACTIVITY AREAS

40

LAUREN HEMP

Playing on the left wing, Lauren Hemp is a nightmare for full-backs to defend against. She dashes forward at every opportunity and has the quick feet to sail past defenders and put a telling pass into the box. She has the courage and physique to outmuscle opponents.

NATIONALITY
English

CURRENT CLUB
Manchester City

11

DATE OF BIRTH	07/08/2000
POSITION	WINGER
HEIGHT	1.64 M
PRO DEBUT	2016
PREFERRED FOOT	LEFT

APPEARANCES
41

DRIBBLES
151

ASSISTS
14

PENALTIES SCORED
0

PASSES
1.212
SUCCESSFUL PASSES
76.3%

GOALS
18

SHOTS
127

CHANCES CREATED
103

TACKLES
51

MAJOR CLUB HONOURS
⚽ Women's FA Cup: 2019
⚽ Women's FA League Cup 2022

INTERNATIONAL HONOURS
⚽ UEFA Women's Championship: 2022
⚽ FIFA Women's World Cup: runner-up 2023
⚽ Women's Finalissima: 2023

ACTIVITY AREAS

26

NATIONALITY
American

CURRENT CLUB
Lyon

LINDSEY HORAN

Lindsey Horan is a creative force in midfield capable of breaking through the back line and getting into forward positions. While she thrives on hitting the net herself, she often takes a split second to scan the pitch for the best option ahead of her. She loves making late runs into the area.

DATE OF BIRTH	26/05/1994
POSITION	ATTACKING
HEIGHT	1.75 M
PRO DEBUT	2012
PREFERRED FOOT	RIGHT

APPEARANCES
46

ASSISTS
8

DRIBBLES
80

PASSES
2.096

SUCCESSFUL PASSES
83.1%

PENALTIES SCORED
0

GOALS
13

SHOTS
122

CHANCES CREATED
60

TACKLES
57

MAJOR CLUB HONOURS
⚽ Division 1 Féminine: 2022, 2023, 2024 ⚽ UEFA Women's Champions League: 2022, runner-up 2024 ⚽ Coupe de France Féminine: 2023 ⚽ NWSL Champions: 2017 (Portland Thorns) ⚽ NWSL Shield: 2016, 2021 (all Portland Thorns) ⚽ NWSL Challenge Cup: 2021 (Portland Thorns FC)

INTERNATIONAL HONOURS
⚽ FIFA Women's World Cup: 2019
⚽ CONCACAF Women's Championship: 2018, 2022
⚽ CONCACAF Women's Gold Cup: 2024

ACTIVITY AREAS

ROSE LAVELLE

Scoring a spectacular goal in the final of a World Cup is the stuff of dreams, but for Rose Lavelle it is part of her amazing success story. She orchestrates quick and free-flowing attacks and is comfortable crossing or shooting with either foot. Her skills are matched by a fiery attitude.

NATIONALITY
American

CURRENT CLUB
NJ/NY Gotham FC

16

DATE OF BIRTH	14/05/1995
POSITION	ATTACKING
HEIGHT	1.62 M
PRO DEBUT	2014
PREFERRED FOOT	LEFT

APPEARANCES
31

ASSISTS
3

DRIBBLES
98

PENALTIES SCORED
0

PASSES
926
SUCCESSFUL PASSES
78.3%

GOALS
7

SHOTS
80

CHANCES CREATED
44

TACKLES
60

MAJOR CLUB HONOURS
⚽ NWSL Shield: 2022 (OL Reign)
⚽ Women's FA Cup: 2020 (Manchester City)

INTERNATIONAL HONOURS
⚽ FIFA Women's World Cup: 2019
⚽ CONCACAF Women's Championship: 2018, 2022
⚽ CONCACAF Women's Gold Cup: 2024

ACTIVITY AREAS

10

NATIONALITY
Scottish

CURRENT CLUB
Arsenal

KIM LITTLE

A model of consistency both in her performances and the desire to win, Kim Little celebrated 300 appearances for Arsenal in 2024. She is a gritty and creative midfielder with a sweet right foot and is ice-cool from the penalty spot.

DATE OF BIRTH	29/06/1990
POSITION	CENTRAL
HEIGHT	1.62 M
PRO DEBUT	2006
PREFERRED FOOT	RIGHT

APPEARANCES
35

ASSISTS
5

DRIBBLES
47

PASSES
1,639

SUCCESSFUL PASSES
87.6%

PENALTIES SCORED
5

GOALS
6

SHOTS
33

CHANCES CREATED
41

TACKLES
48

MAJOR CLUB HONOURS
⚽ Women's Super League: 2011, 2012, 2019 ⚽ Women's FA Cup: 2009, 2011, 2013 ⚽ Women's FA League Cup: 2011, 2012, 2013, 2018, 2023, 2024 ⚽ NWSL Shield: 2014, 2015 (all Seattle Reign) ⚽ A-League Champions: 2016 (Melbourne City) ⚽ A-League Premiership: 2016 (Melbourne City)

INTERNATIONAL HONOURS
⚽ None to date

ACTIVITY AREAS

VICKY LÓPEZ

The skill, maturity and finishing ability of this teenager is frightening. When attacking Vicky López has the power and athleticism to skip past defenders and line up a shot. Besides her talent in front of goal, her link-up play and pressing are top class.

NATIONALITY
Spanish

CURRENT CLUB
Barcelona

30

DATE OF BIRTH	26/06/2006
POSITION	ATTACKING
HEIGHT	1.61 M
PRO DEBUT	2021
PREFERRED FOOT	RIGHT

APPEARANCES
40

ASSISTS
3

DRIBBLES
54

PENALTIES SCORED
0

PASSES
1,014
SUCCESSFUL PASSES
83.2%

GOALS
10

SHOTS
58

CHANCES CREATED
25

TACKLES
38

MAJOR CLUB HONOURS
⊕ Liga F: 2023, 2024
⚽ UEFA Women's Champions League: 2023, 2024
⊕ Copa de la Reina: 2024

INTERNATIONAL HONOURS
⚽ UEFA Women's Nations League: 2024

ACTIVITY AREAS

12

NATIONALITY
Norwegian

CURRENT CLUB
Arsenal

FRIDA MAANUM

Expect to see Frida Maanum driving her team forward, from deep midfield or a more attacking position. Her sharp footwork helps her wriggle free from challenges and she is not afraid to shoot from distance. She is one of the finest free-kick takers in the WSL.

DATE OF BIRTH	16/07/1999
POSITION	CENTRAL
HEIGHT	1.71 M
PRO DEBUT	2014
PREFERRED FOOT	RIGHT

ASSISTS
7

APPEARANCES
53

DRIBBLES
100

PENALTIES SCORED
0

PASSES
1,280
SUCCESSFUL PASSES
79.3%

GOALS
17

SHOTS
132

CHANCES CREATED
78

TACKLES
37

MAJOR CLUB HONOURS
⚽ FA Women's League Cup: 2023, 2024

INTERNATIONAL HONOURS
⚽ None to date

ACTIVITY AREAS

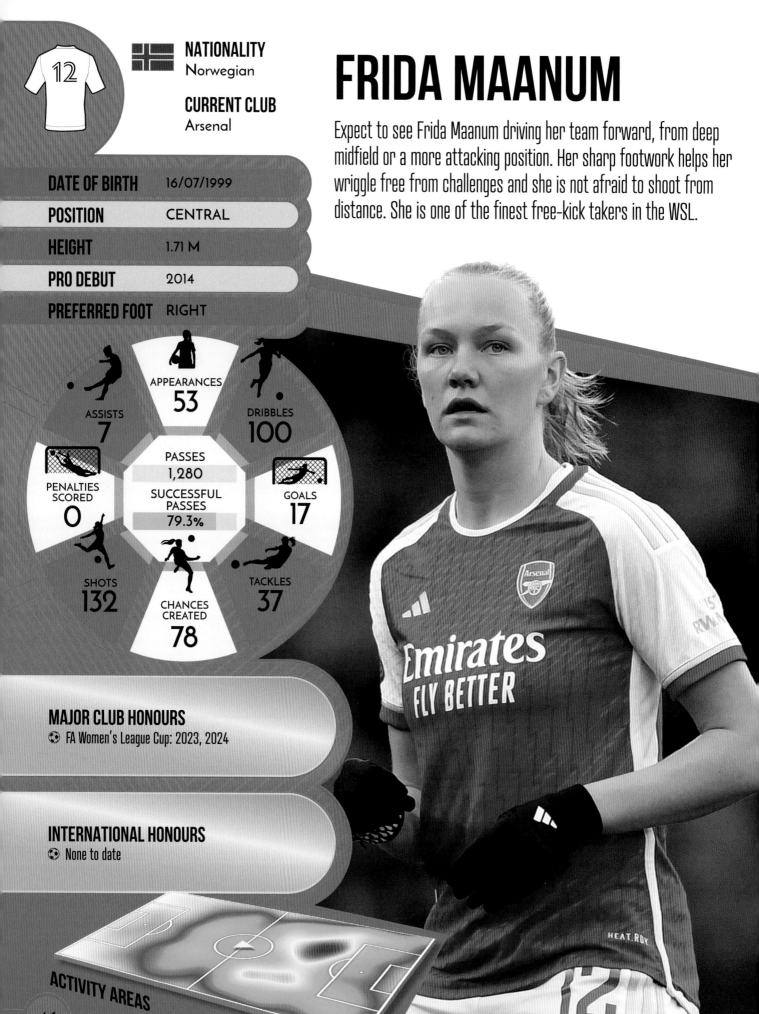

LIEKE MARTENS

Lieke Martens is right footed and usually plays on the left wing, allowing her to cut inside and unleash accurate shots and passes. If the ball drops around the box, she can blast at goal with little back lift. Her volleying technique is among the very best.

NATIONALITY
Dutch

CURRENT CLUB
Paris Saint-Germain

11

DATE OF BIRTH	16/12/1992
POSITION	WINGER
HEIGHT	1.70 M
PRO DEBUT	2009
PREFERRED FOOT	RIGHT

APPEARANCES
45

ASSISTS
5

DRIBBLES
66

PASSES
1,051

PENALTIES SCORED
0

SUCCESSFUL PASSES
81.4%

GOALS
6

SHOTS
82

CHANCES CREATED
41

TACKLES
19

MAJOR CLUB HONOURS
⚽ Liga F: 2020, 2021, 2022 (all Barcelona)
⚽ UEFA Women's Champions League: 2021 (Barcelona)
⚽ Copa de la Reina: 2018, 2020, 2021, 2022 (all Barcelona)

INTERNATIONAL HONOURS
⚽ UEFA Women's Championship: 2017
⚽ FIFA Women's World Cup: runner-up 2019

ACTIVITY AREAS

47

20

NATIONALITY
Japanese

CURRENT CLUB
Manchester United

HINATA MIYAZAWA

With her speed and cool finishing, Hinata Miyazawa does a superb job of supporting the forwards and increasing her team's attacking options. Adept with either foot, she weaves clever passes and cracks shots off with ease. She was the top scorer at the 2023 World Cup.

DATE OF BIRTH	28/11/1999
POSITION	ATTACKING
HEIGHT	1.60 M
PRO DEBUT	2018
PREFERRED FOOT	RIGHT

APPEARANCES
12

ASSISTS
1

DRIBBLES
6

PASSES
235

SUCCESSFUL PASSES
84.3%

PENALTIES SCORED
0

GOALS
1

SHOTS
19

TACKLES
8

CHANCES CREATED
8

MAJOR CLUB HONOURS
⚽ AFC Women's Club Championship: 2019
   (Tokyo Verdy Beleza)
⚽ Women's FA Cup: 2024

INTERNATIONAL HONOURS
⚽ None to date

ACTIVITY AREAS

48

LENA OBERDORF

Hailed as one of the best young defensive midfielders in Europe, Lena Oberdorf was snapped up by top side Bayern Munich in 2024. A natural leader who demands high standards, she enjoys pressing and tackling and when space opens up she has the ability to power forward.

NATIONALITY
German

CURRENT CLUB
Bayern Munich

*TBC

DATE OF BIRTH	19/12/2001
POSITION	DEFENSIVE
HEIGHT	1.74 M
PRO DEBUT	2018
PREFERRED FOOT	RIGHT

APPEARANCES
42

ASSISTS
5

DRIBBLES
47

PASSES
1,631

SUCCESSFUL PASSES
71.5%

PENALTIES SCORED
0

GOALS
8

SHOTS
49

TACKLES
144

CHANCES CREATED
34

MAJOR CLUB HONOURS
⚽ Frauen-Bundesliga: 2022 (VfL Wolfsburg)
⚽ DFB-Pokal Frauen: 2021, 2022, 2023, 2024

INTERNATIONAL HONOURS
⚽ UEFA Women's Championship: runner-up 2022

ACTIVITY AREAS

NATIONALITY
Spanish

CURRENT CLUB
Barcelona

CLÀUDIA PINA

Able to operate as a midfielder or forward, Barcelona's prolific number six has unique attributes that make her a world-class player. Clàudia Pina appears in pockets of space as she probes and passes towards goal, bamboozling even the most disciplined defences.

DATE OF BIRTH	12/08/2001
POSITION	ATTACKING
HEIGHT	1.60 M
PRO DEBUT	2016
PREFERRED FOOT	RIGHT

APPEARANCES
65

ASSISTS
18

DRIBBLES
80

PASSES
2,103

SUCCESSFUL PASSES
84.4%

PENALTIES SCORED
2

GOALS
26

SHOTS
176

TACKLES
55

CHANCES CREATED
125

MAJOR CLUB HONOURS
⚽ Liga F: 2020, 2022, 2023, 2024
⚽ UEFA Champions League: 2023, 2024
⚽ Copa de la Reina: 2020, 2022, 2024

INTERNATIONAL HONOURS
⚽ None to date

ACTIVITY AREAS

ALEXIA PUTELLAS

Barcelona's decorated midfielder is arguably today's most influential player for both club and country. Her positional play and attacking instincts are matched by her high-octane defensive work. Alexia Putellas makes ghosting beyond an opponent and hitting a raking pass look so simple.

NATIONALITY
Spanish

CURRENT CLUB
Barcelona

11

DATE OF BIRTH	04/02/1994
POSITION	ATTACKING
HEIGHT	1.73 M
PRO DEBUT	2008
PREFERRED FOOT	LEFT

APPEARANCES
30

ASSISTS
5

DRIBBLES
44

PASSES
992

SUCCESSFUL PASSES
83.8%

PENALTIES SCORED
2

GOALS
12

SHOTS
69

CHANCES CREATED
44

TACKLES
24

MAJOR CLUB HONOURS
⚽ Liga F: 2013, 2014, 2015, 2020, 2021, 2022, 2023, 2024
⚽ UEFA Women's Champions League: 2021, 2023, 2024
⚽ Copa de la Reina: 2013, 2014, 2017, 2018, 2020, 2021, 2022, 2024

INTERNATIONAL HONOURS
⚽ FIFA Women's World Cup: 2023
⚽ UEFA Women's Nations League: 2024

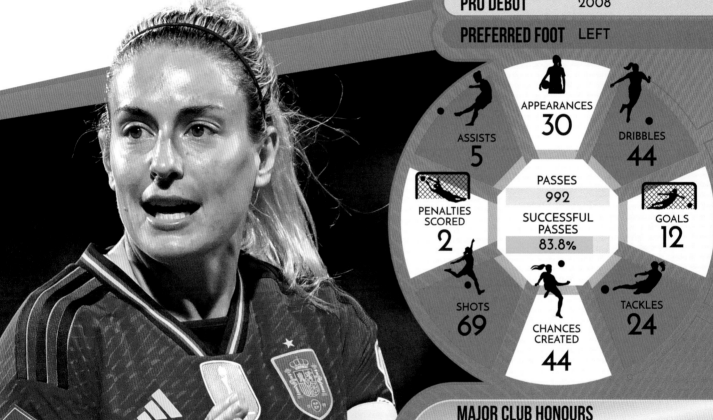

ACTIVITY AREAS

11

NATIONALITY
Norwegian

CURRENT CLUB
Chelsea

GURO REITEN

Some wingers drift out of games as they wait for the ball. Not Guro Reiten. The left-footed Chelsea favourite enjoys taking possession and dribbling at speed or leaving opponents dazed with one instinctive flick. Her forward raids rarely fail.

DATE OF BIRTH	26/07/1994
POSITION	WINGER
HEIGHT	1.67 M
PRO DEBUT	2010
PREFERRED FOOT	LEFT

APPEARANCES
55

ASSISTS
23

DRIBBLES
74

PASSES
1,293
SUCCESSFUL PASSES
67.8%

PENALTIES SCORED
6

GOALS
20

SHOTS
85

CHANCES CREATED
121

TACKLES
45

MAJOR CLUB HONOURS
⚽ Women's Super League: 2020, 2021, 2022, 2023, 2024 ⚽ UEFA Women's Champions League: runner-up 2021 ⚽ Women's FA Cup: 2021, 2022, 2023 ⚽ Women's FA League Cup: 2020, 2021

INTERNATIONAL HONOURS
⚽ None to date

ACTIVITY AREAS

GEORGIA STANWAY

Georgia Stanway's influence may go unnoticed in central midfield but do not underestimate her importance. In transitions, her ability to win second balls and fly into tackles can be the difference between victory and defeat. She is hugely competitive with a strong will to win.

NATIONALITY
English

CURRENT CLUB
Bayern Munich

31

DATE OF BIRTH	03/01/1999
POSITION	CENTRAL
HEIGHT	1.64 M
PRO DEBUT	2015
PREFERRED FOOT	RIGHT

APPEARANCES
56

ASSISTS
10

DRIBBLES
127

PENALTIES SCORED
4

PASSES
3,827
SUCCESSFUL PASSES
84.9%

GOALS
15

SHOTS
109

CHANCES CREATED
80

TACKLES
115

MAJOR CLUB HONOURS
⚽ Frauen-Bundesliga: 2023, 2024 ⚽ Women's Super League: 2016 (Manchester City) ⚽ Women's FA Cup: 2017, 2019, 2020 (Manchester City) ⚽ Women's FA League Cup: 2016, 2019, 2022 (Manchester City)

INTERNATIONAL HONOURS
⚽ UEFA Women's Championship: 2022
⚽ FIFA Women's World Cup: runner-up 2023
⚽ Women's Finalissima: 2023

ACTIVITY AREAS

7

ELLA TOONE

Goals, assists and world-class performances are what Ella Toone has in her locker. An intelligent midfielder who sits off the forwards, she makes telling contributions with her energy, technique and visionary passing. 'Tooney' can lift her team-mates and the crowd with one magic moment.

DATE OF BIRTH	02/09/1999
POSITION	CENTRAL
HEIGHT	1.63 M
PRO DEBUT	2015
PREFERRED FOOT	RIGHT

APPEARANCES
44

ASSISTS
12

DRIBBLES
62

PASSES
1,729

SUCCESSFUL PASSES
79.2%

PENALTIES SCORED
0

GOALS
9

SHOTS
75

TACKLES
33

CHANCES CREATED
75

MAJOR CLUB HONOURS
⚽ Women's Super League: 2016 (Manchester City) ⚽ FA Women's Championship: 2019 ⚽ Women's FA Cup: 2024 ⚽ Women's FA League Cup: 2016 (Manchester City)

INTERNATIONAL HONOURS
⚽ UEFA Women's Championship: 2022
⚽ Women's Finalissima: 2023
⚽ FIFA Women's World Cup: runner-up 2023

ACTIVITY AREAS

DANIËLLE VAN DE DONK

Thanks to her vision and experience, Daniëlle van de Donk creates scoring chances that frequently hurt the opposition. Efficient with her tackling and passing, she loves going forward, ready to fire a right-footed shot. Her heading is another top skill.

NATIONALITY
Dutch

CURRENT CLUB
Lyon

DATE OF BIRTH	05/08/1991
POSITION	CENTRAL
HEIGHT	1.60 M
PRO DEBUT	2008
PREFERRED FOOT	RIGHT

APPEARANCES
57

DRIBBLES
73

ASSISTS
7

PASSES
1,712

SUCCESSFUL PASSES
81.5%

GOALS
9

PENALTIES SCORED
0

SHOTS
82

CHANCES CREATED
62

TACKLES
80

MAJOR CLUB HONOURS
- Division 1 Féminine: 2022, 2023, 2024
- UEFA Women's Champions League: 2022, runner-up 2024
- Women's FA Cup: 2016 (Arsenal)

INTERNATIONAL HONOURS
- UEFA Women's Championship: 2017
- FIFA Women's World Cup: 2019

ACTIVITY AREAS

21

NATIONALITY
English

CURRENT CLUB
Barcelona

KEIRA WALSH

Keira Walsh disrupts opponents in central areas and recycles the ball superbly. More than just a defensive player, her forward passes and intelligent movement expands her team's options. Vocal and powerful yet always in control.

DATE OF BIRTH	08/04/1997
POSITION	DEFENSIVE
HEIGHT	1.65 M
PRO DEBUT	2014
PREFERRED FOOT	RIGHT

APPEARANCES
68

ASSISTS
6

DRIBBLES
33

PASSES
3,905

SUCCESSFUL PASSES
92.4%

PENALTIES SCORED
0

GOALS
3

SHOTS
20

CHANCES CREATED
58

TACKLES
74

MAJOR CLUB HONOURS
⚽ Liga F: 2023, 2024 ⚽ UEFA Champions League: 2023, 2024 ⚽ Women's Super League: 2016 ⚽ Copa de la Reina: 2024 ⚽ Women's FA Cup: 2017, 2019, 2020 ⚽ Women's FA League Cup: 2014, 2016, 2019, 2022 (all Manchester City)

INTERNATIONAL HONOURS
⚽ UEFA Women's Championship: 2022
⚽ Women's Finalissima: 2023
⚽ FIFA Women's World Cup: runner-up 2023

ACTIVITY AREAS

CAROLINE WEIR

Tall, agile, strong and with a left foot that does special things, Caroline Weir sparkles in her attacking midfield duties. Her coaches love how she shoots and hits the target from long range, plus when she connects beautifully with crosses. She offers the complete package.

NATIONALITY
Scottish

CURRENT CLUB
Real Madrid

10

DATE OF BIRTH	20/06/1995
POSITION	ATTACKING
HEIGHT	1.73 M
PRO DEBUT	2011
PREFERRED FOOT	LEFT

APPEARANCES
34

ASSISTS
12

DRIBBLES
86

PASSES
1,424

SUCCESSFUL PASSES
87.3%

PENALTIES SCORED
0

GOALS
21

SHOTS
108

CHANCES CREATED
93

TACKLES
36

MAJOR CLUB HONOURS
⚽ Women's FA Cup: 2014 (Arsenal), 2019,* 2020* (*Manchester City), ⚽ Women's FA League Cup: 2019, 2020 (all Manchester City)

INTERNATIONAL HONOURS
⚽ None to date

ACTIVITY AREAS

FORWARDS

The players who usually make the most headlines are the forwards. Also known as strikers, their task is to do the most important thing in football — score goals! Forwards need a range of skills to do this, from accurate shooting to brave heading and well-timed runs into the penalty box. These players can be big and strong or small and quick. Sometimes they play in a striking pair or as a trio, or other times they lead the attack on their own. Forwards love being the hero when they hit the back of the net.

WHAT DO THE STATS MEAN?

GOALS
This is the total number of goals a forward has scored. The figure spans across all the top clubs the player has represented in the pas two seasons

ASSISTS
A pass, cross or header to a teammate who then scores counts as an assist. This stat also includes a deflected shot that is immediately converted by a teammate.

 75%

CONVERSION RATE
The percentage shows how good the player is at taking their chance in front of goal. If a player scores two goals from four shots, their conversion rate is 50 per cent.

128

MINUTES PER GOAL
This is the average length of time it takes for the player to score. It is calculated across all the minutes the player has played in the past two seasons at top level.

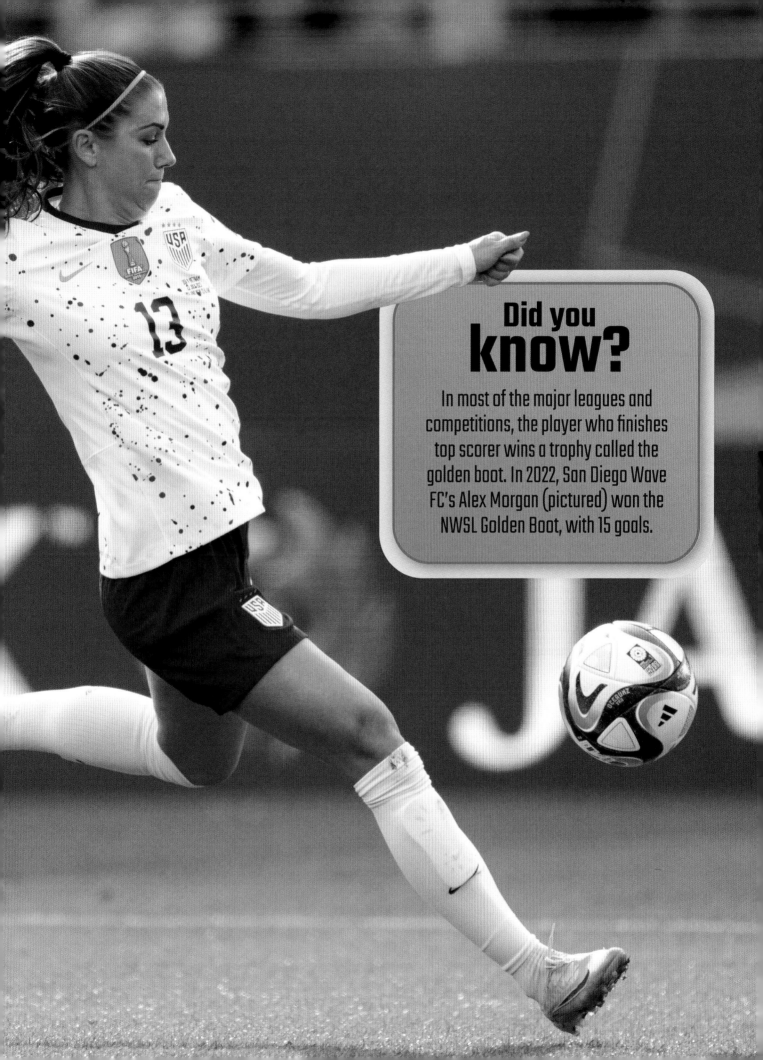

Did you know?

In most of the major leagues and competitions, the player who finishes top scorer wins a trophy called the golden boot. In 2022, San Diego Wave FC's Alex Morgan (pictured) won the NWSL Golden Boot, with 15 goals.

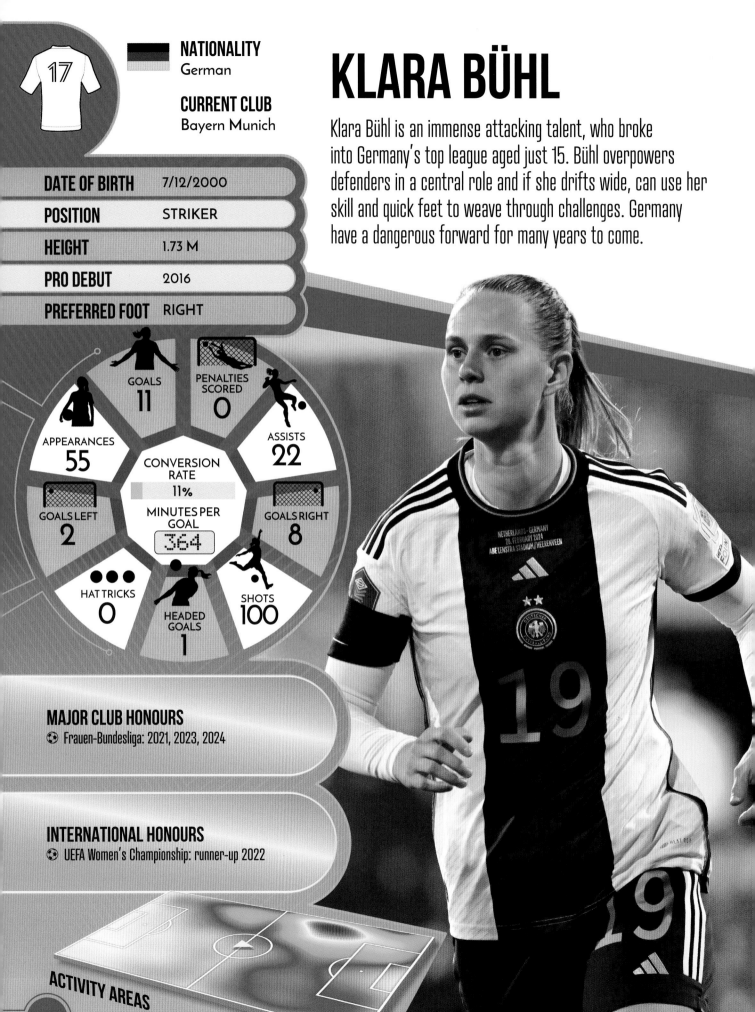

17

KLARA BÜHL

Klara Bühl is an immense attacking talent, who broke into Germany's top league aged just 15. Bühl overpowers defenders in a central role and if she drifts wide, can use her skill and quick feet to weave through challenges. Germany have a dangerous forward for many years to come.

DATE OF BIRTH	7/12/2000
POSITION	STRIKER
HEIGHT	1.73 M
PRO DEBUT	2016
PREFERRED FOOT	RIGHT

GOALS
11

PENALTIES SCORED
0

ASSISTS
22

APPEARANCES
55

CONVERSION RATE
11%

GOALS LEFT
2

MINUTES PER GOAL
364

GOALS RIGHT
8

HAT TRICKS
0

HEADED GOALS
1

SHOTS
100

MAJOR CLUB HONOURS
⚽ Frauen-Bundesliga: 2021, 2023, 2024

INTERNATIONAL HONOURS
⚽ UEFA Women's Championship: runner-up 2022

ACTIVITY AREAS

KADIDIATOU DIANI

Kadidiatou Diani is a huge threat in attacking areas. Not only is she clinical inside the box but her dribbling and speed allow her to open up opportunities for her team. As she proved at the 2023 World Cup, where she was the second highest goalscorer, Diani rises for the big occasion.

NATIONALITY
France

CURRENT CLUB
Lyon

11

DATE OF BIRTH	01/04/1995
POSITION	FORWARD
HEIGHT	1.69 M
PRO DEBUT	2011
PREFERRED FOOT	RIGHT

GOALS
36

PENALTIES SCORED
7

ASSISTS
16

APPEARANCES
53

CONVERSION RATE
22.5%

MINUTES PER GOAL
108

GOALS LEFT
3

GOALS RIGHT
24

HAT TRICKS
1

HEADED GOALS
8

SHOTS
160

MAJOR CLUB HONOURS
- Division 1 Féminine: 2021 (PSG), 2024
- UEFA Champions League: runner-up 2024
- Coupe de France Féminine: 2018, 2022 (ali PSG)

INTERNATIONAL HONOURS
- None to date

ACTIVITY AREAS

61

19

NATIONALITY
Australian

CURRENT CLUB
Arsenal

CAITLIN FOORD

Caitlin Foord is known for her inspirational moments for club and country. Whether playing wide on either flank or through the centre, Foord's attacking flair and hunger for goals so often get her team on top. From range or close in, she knows how to hit the net.

DATE OF BIRTH	11/11/1994
POSITION	FORWARD
HEIGHT	1.65 M
PRO DEBUT	2009
PREFERRED FOOT	RIGHT

GOALS
14

PENALTIES SCORED
0

APPEARANCES
48

ASSISTS
12

CONVERSION RATE
11.3%

GOALS LEFT
3

MINUTES PER GOAL
252

GOALS RIGHT
9

HAT TRICKS
0

HEADED GOALS
2

SHOTS
124

MAJOR CLUB HONOURS
- A-League Premiership: 2011 (Sydney FC), 2014 (Perth Glory)
- A-League Championship: 2013, 2019 (Sydney FC)
- Women's FA League Cup: 2023, 2024

INTERNATIONAL HONOURS
- None to date

ACTIVITY AREAS

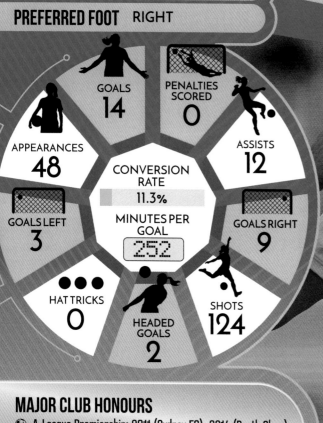

CAROLINE GRAHAM HANSEN

NATIONALITY
Norwegian

CURRENT CLUB
Barcelona

Caroline Graham Hansen is a natural goalscorer and one of the finest dribblers around, which are two reasons why she has the honour of wearing Barcelona's number 10 shirt. She's known for slaloming past defenders and delivering clever passes and crosses. Graham hasn't even reached her peak yet.

DATE OF BIRTH	18/02/1995
POSITION	FORWARD
HEIGHT	1.75 M
PRO DEBUT	2010
PREFERRED FOOT	RIGHT

GOALS 37
PENALTIES SCORED 1
ASSISTS 32
APPEARANCES 52
CONVERSION RATE 19.4%
MINUTES PER GOAL 99
GOALS LEFT 11
GOALS RIGHT 24
HAT TRICKS 1
HEADED GOALS 2
SHOTS 191

MAJOR CLUB HONOURS
- ⚽ Liga F: 2020, 2021, 2022, 2023, 2024
- ⚽ UEFA Women's Champions League: 2021, 2023, 2024
- ⚽ Frauen Bundesliga: 2017, 2018, 2019 (all VfL Wolfsburg)

INTERNATIONAL HONOURS
- ⚽ UEFA Women's Championship: runner-up 2013

ACTIVITY AREAS

21

NATIONALITY
Danish

CURRENT CLUB
Bayern Munich

PERNILLE HARDER

Able to finish with her right or left foot, Pernille Harder is a slick and versatile attacker. The Denmark captain drives into space with her powerful runs and has the coolness and vision to execute a shot or assist. She is very capable from free-kicks and headers too.

DATE OF BIRTH	15/11/1992
POSITION	FORWARD
HEIGHT	1.69 M
PRO DEBUT	2007
PREFERRED FOOT	BOTH

GOALS
20

PENALTIES SCORED
1

ASSISTS
9

APPEARANCES
32

CONVERSION RATE
20.4%

MINUTES PER GOAL
107

GOALS LEFT
3

GOALS RIGHT
14

HAT TRICKS
2

HEADED GOALS
3

SHOTS
98

MAJOR CLUB HONOURS
⚽ Frauen-Bundesliga: 2017, 2018, 2019, 2020 (all VfL Wolfsburg), 2024
⚽ DFB-Pokal Frauen: 2017, 2018, 2019, 2020 (all VfL Wolfsburg) ⚽ Women's Super League: 2021, 2022, 2023 (all Chelsea) ⚽ Women's FA Cup: 2021, 2022, 2023 (all Chelsea) ⚽ UEFA Women's Champions League: runner-up 2021 (Chelsea) runner-up 2018*, 2020* (*VfL Wolfsburg)

INTERNATIONAL HONOURS
⚽ UEFA Women's Championship: runner-up 2017

ACTIVITY AREAS

ADA HEGERBERG

Ada Hegerberg is among the most accomplished players in the women's game! As well as winning multiple team trophies, the prolific striker is the leading UEFA Champions League scorer with more than 60 goals and was the first Ballon d'Or Féminin winner in 2018. She has been a world-class player for more than a decade.

NATIONALITY
Norwegian

CURRENT CLUB
Lyon

14

DATE OF BIRTH	10/07/1995
POSITION	STRIKER
HEIGHT	1.76 M
PRO DEBUT	2010
PREFERRED FOOT	RIGHT

GOALS
21

PENALTIES SCORED
3

ASSISTS
3

APPEARANCES
28

CONVERSION RATE
20.6%

MINUTES PER GOAL
73

GOALS LEFT
5

GOALS RIGHT
16

HAT TRICKS
3

HEADED GOALS
0

SHOTS
102

MAJOR CLUB HONOURS
⚽ Division 1 Féminine: 2015, 2016, 2017, 2018, 2019, 2020, 2022, 2023, 2024 ⚽ UEFA Women's Champions League: 2016, 2017, 2018, 2019, 2020, 2022, runner-up 2024 ⚽ Coupe de France Féminine: 2015, 2016, 2017, 2019, 2020, 2023

INTERNATIONAL HONOURS
⚽ UEFA Women's Championship: runner-up 2013

ACTIVITY AREAS

23

NATIONALITY
Australian

CURRENT CLUB
Canberra United

MICHELLE HEYMAN

In 2024, prolific striker Michelle Heyman was the first to net 100 A-League goals and made a scoring return for Australia to help her side qualify for the Paris Olympics. She can rip through back lines with her sharp movement while her height gives her an advantage against defenders.

DATE OF BIRTH	04/07/1988
POSITION	STRIKER
HEIGHT	1.80 M
PRO DEBUT	2008
PREFERRED FOOT	RIGHT

GOALS
29

PENALTIES SCORED
0

APPEARANCES
40

ASSISTS
10

CONVERSION RATE
22.5%

MINUTES PER GOAL
117

GOALS LEFT
6

GOALS RIGHT
18

HAT TRICKS
1

HEADED GOALS
4

SHOTS
129

MAJOR CLUB HONOURS
⚽ A-League Premiership: 2012, 2014
⚽ A-League Championship: 2012, 2014

INTERNATIONAL HONOURS
⚽ None to date

ACTIVITY AREAS

LAUREN JAMES

One of the breakout stars at the 2023 World Cup, Lauren James is capable of spectacular goals and assists. She often plays in wide positions and cuts inside to shoot or finds a pass with either foot. One of her trademark finishes is to bend the ball inside the far post from range.

NATIONALITY
English

CURRENT CLUB
Chelsea

17

DATE OF BIRTH	29/09/2001
POSITION	FORWARD
HEIGHT	1.75 M
PRO DEBUT	2017
PREFERRED FOOT	RIGHT

GOALS
21

PENALTIES SCORED
0

ASSISTS
5

APPEARANCES
50

CONVERSION RATE
14.8%

MINUTES PER GOAL
156

GOALS LEFT
10

GOALS RIGHT
11

HAT TRICKS
2

HEADED GOALS
0

SHOTS
142

MAJOR CLUB HONOURS
⚽ FA Women's Super League: 2022, 2023, 2024
⚽ FA Women's Cup: 2022, 2023

INTERNATIONAL HONOURS
⚽ FIFA Women's World Cup: runner-up 2023
⚽ FIFA Women's Finalissima: 2023

ACTIVITY AREAS

20

NATIONALITY
Australian

CURRENT CLUB
Chelsea

SAM KERR

Australia's Sam Kerr is regarded as one of the best strikers ever since she burst onto the scene as a teenager! She uses her speed and positional sense to unlock defences and is clinical in front of goal. She is a spectacular finisher, famous for her volleys, lobs and long-range rockets. A true legend of the game.

DATE OF BIRTH	10/09/1993
POSITION	STRIKER
HEIGHT	1.68 M
PRO DEBUT	2008
PREFERRED FOOT	RIGHT

GOALS
26

PENALTIES SCORED
0

ASSISTS
10

APPEARANCES
43

CONVERSION RATE
17.1%

MINUTES PER GOAL
129

GOALS LEFT
4

GOALS RIGHT
15

HAT TRICKS
2

HEADED GOALS
7

SHOTS
152

MAJOR CLUB HONOURS
⚽ Women's Super League: 2020, 2021, 2022, 2023, 2024 ⚽ Women's FA Cup: 2021, 2022, 2023 ⚽ UEFA Women's Champions League: runner-up 2021 ⚽ A-League Championship: 2013 (Sydney FC) ⚽ NWSL Shield: 2013 (Western New York Flash) ⚽ A-League Premiership: 2014 (Perth Glory)

INTERNATIONAL HONOURS
⚽ AFC Women's Asian Cup: 2010

ACTIVITY AREAS

RACHEAL KUNDANANJI

Joining Bay FC for a record fee of £625,000 in 2024, Racheal Kundananji is a thrilling forward. She is super confident in possession and spins clear of her marker to connect with crosses and passes. Kundananji's technique and timing inside the box mean she needs only a sniff of a chance to beat a goalkeeper.

NATIONALITY
Zambian

CURRENT CLUB
Bay FC

9

DATE OF BIRTH	03/06/2000
POSITION	FORWARD
HEIGHT	1.70 M
PRO DEBUT	2018
PREFERRED FOOT	RIGHT

GOALS
37

PENALTIES SCORED
0

ASSISTS
7

APPEARANCES
58

CONVERSION RATE
18.2%

GOALS LEFT
14

MINUTES PER GOAL
122

GOALS RIGHT
20

HAT TRICKS
2

HEADED GOALS
3

SHOTS
203

MAJOR CLUB HONOURS
⚽ FAZ Women Super League: 2018 (Indeni Roses)
⚽ Kazakhstani Championship: 2019, 2020
(all BIIK Kazygurt)

INTERNATIONAL HONOURS
⚽ None to date

ACTIVITY AREAS

NATIONALITY
France

CURRENT CLUB
Lyon

EUGÉNIE LE SOMMER

Eugénie Le Sommer is into the 17th season of a prolific career and remains a potent force in front of goal. The record scorer for France and Lyon, she is so difficult to stop as she powers into the box and blasts, curls or chips into the net. Le Sommer is an icon of the game.

DATE OF BIRTH	18/05/1989
POSITION	FORWARD
HEIGHT	1.61 M
PRO DEBUT	2007
PREFERRED FOOT	RIGHT

GOALS
18

PENALTIES SCORED
0

ASSISTS
10

APPEARANCES
45

CONVERSION RATE
15.7%

MINUTES PER GOAL
145

GOALS LEFT
8

GOALS RIGHT
7

HAT TRICKS
0

HEADED GOALS
3

SHOTS
115

MAJOR CLUB HONOURS
⚽ Division 1 Féminine: 2011-2020, 2022, 2023, 2024 ⚽
UEFA Women's Champions League: 2011, 2012, 2016, 2017,
2018, 2019, 2020, 2022, runner-up 2024 ⚽ Coupe de
France Féminine: 2012-2017, 2019, 2020, 2023

INTERNATIONAL HONOURS
⚽ SheBelieves Cup: 2017

ACTIVITY AREAS

BETH MEAD

Beth Mead is a gamechanger in her favoured right-sided role. Playing on the shoulder of defenders, she can trap the ball and turn to run into space or chase it in the channels and link up with other attackers. Her 33 goals in her first 56 England games justifies her world-class status.

NATIONALITY
English

CURRENT CLUB
Arsenal

9

DATE OF BIRTH	09/05/1995
POSITION	FORWARD
HEIGHT	1.63 M
PRO DEBUT	2011
PREFERRED FOOT	RIGHT

GOALS
13

PENALTIES SCORED
0

APPEARANCES
29

ASSISTS
9

CONVERSION RATE
18.3%

GOALS LEFT
3

MINUTES PER GOAL
165

GOALS RIGHT
9

HAT TRICKS
0

HEADED GOALS
1

SHOTS
71

MAJOR CLUB HONOURS
- Women's Super League: 2019
- Women's FA League Cup: 2018, 2023, 2024

INTERNATIONAL HONOURS
- UEFA Women's Championship: 2022

ACTIVITY AREAS

NATIONALITY
Dutch

CURRENT CLUB
TBC

VIVIANNE MIEDEMA

Scorer of a record 100 goals in only 110 games during her time at Arsenal highlights just how ruthless Vivianne Miedema is in front of goal. Tall, physical and equally skilful on the deck as she is in the air, the Dutch legend has all the tricks and powers required to hurt the opposition.

DATE OF BIRTH	15/07/1996
POSITION	STRIKER
HEIGHT	1.77 M
PRO DEBUT	2011
PREFERRED FOOT	RIGHT

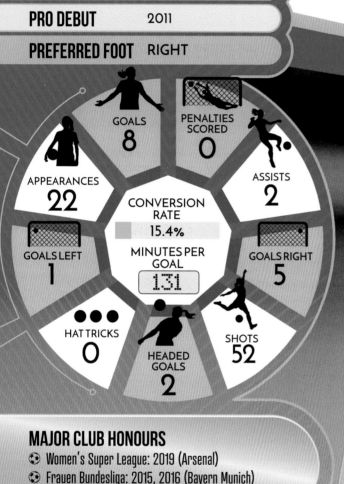

GOALS
8

PENALTIES SCORED
0

APPEARANCES
22

ASSISTS
2

CONVERSION RATE
15.4%

MINUTES PER GOAL
131

GOALS LEFT
1

GOALS RIGHT
5

HAT TRICKS
0

HEADED GOALS
2

SHOTS
52

MAJOR CLUB HONOURS
- Women's Super League: 2019 (Arsenal)
- Frauen Bundesliga: 2015, 2016 (Bayern Munich)
- Women's FA League Cup: 2018, 2023, 2024 (Arsenal)

INTERNATIONAL HONOURS
- UEFA Women's Championship: 2017
- FIFA Women's World Cup: runner-up 2019

ACTIVITY AREAS

ALEX MORGAN

Two-time FIFA World Cup winner Alex Morgan is at her best leading the striking line and showcasing her shooting confidence. Whether controlling cross-field passes in the area or running behind defenders, Morgan's desire to score means the opposition always have to mark her closely.

NATIONALITY
American

CURRENT CLUB
San Diego Wave

DATE OF BIRTH	02/07/1989
POSITION	STRIKER
HEIGHT	1.70 M
PRO DEBUT	2008
PREFERRED FOOT	LEFT

GOALS
23

PENALTIES SCORED
7

APPEARANCES
43

ASSISTS
9

CONVERSION RATE
16%

MINUTES PER GOAL
158

GOALS LEFT
17

GOALS RIGHT
4

HAT TRICKS
1

HEADED GOALS
2

SHOTS
143

MAJOR CLUB HONOURS
⚽ NWSL Shield: 2023 ⚽ NWSL Championship: 2013 (Portland Thorns) ⚽ UEFA Women's Champions League: 2017 (Lyon) ⚽ Division 1 Féminine: 2017 (Lyon) ⚽ Coupe de France Féminine: 2017 (Lyon)

INTERNATIONAL HONOURS
⚽ FIFA Women's World Cup: 2015, 2019 ⚽ Olympic Games: 2012 ⚽ CONCACAF Women's Championship: 2014, 2018, 2022 ⚽ CONCACAF Women's Gold Cup: 2024

ACTIVITY AREAS

NATIONALITY
French

CURRENT CLUB
VfL Wolfsburg

EWA PAJOR

Poland's most potent female forward, Ewa Pajor scores headers, long-range goals and accurate tap-ins at a prolific rate. She runs rampant in the German league and European competitions as she bullies defenders and finds space to let fly with her dangerous right foot.

DATE OF BIRTH	03/12/1996
POSITION	STRIKER
HEIGHT	1.67 M
PRO DEBUT	2012
PREFERRED FOOT	RIGHT

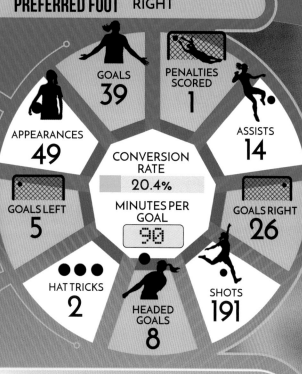

GOALS
39

PENALTIES SCORED
1

APPEARANCES
49

ASSISTS
14

CONVERSION RATE
20.4%

MINUTES PER GOAL
90

GOALS LEFT
5

GOALS RIGHT
26

HAT TRICKS
2

HEADED GOALS
8

SHOTS
191

MAJOR CLUB HONOURS
⚽ Frauen-Bundesliga: 2017, 2018, 2019, 2020, 2022
⚽ UEFA Women's Champions League: runner-up* 2016*, 2018*, 2020*, 2023* ⚽ DFB-Pokal Frauen: 2016, 2017, 2018, 2019, 2020, 2021, 2022, 2023, 2024

INTERNATIONAL HONOURS
⚽ None to date

ACTIVITY AREAS

SALMA PARALLUELO

Just 19 when she won the World Cup, scooping up the tournament's Best Young Player award too, Salma Paralluelo has had a spectacular start to her career. Her mind-blowing dribbles into the penalty box, defence-splitting passes and crosses put her among the world's very best attackers.

NATIONALITY
Spanish

CURRENT CLUB
Barcelona

7

DATE OF BIRTH	13/01/2003
POSITION	FORWARD
HEIGHT	1.75 M
PRO DEBUT	2019
PREFERRED FOOT	LEFT

GOALS
36

PENALTIES SCORED
0

ASSISTS
9

APPEARANCES
56

CONVERSION RATE
22.2%

MINUTES PER GOAL
98

GOALS LEFT
25

GOALS RIGHT
8

HAT TRICKS
2

HEADED GOALS
3

SHOTS
162

MAJOR CLUB HONOURS
- Liga F: 2023, 2024
- UEFA Women's Champions League: 2023, 2024
- Copa de la Reina: 2024

INTERNATIONAL HONOURS
- FIFA Women's World Cup: 2023
- UEFA Women's Nations League: 2024

ACTIVITY AREAS

11

NATIONALITY
German

CURRENT CLUB
VfL Wolfsburg

ALEXANDRA POPP

Alexandra Popp has one of the most cultured left-footed shots in European football. A natural leader for club and country, her aggression and passion are matched on the pitch by skill and creativity. Popp can burst through any defence and calmly put the ball past the goalkeeper.

DATE OF BIRTH	06/04/1991
POSITION	STRIKER
HEIGHT	1.74 M
PRO DEBUT	2007
PREFERRED FOOT	LEFT

GOALS
26

PENALTIES SCORED
0

APPEARANCES
50

ASSISTS
15

CONVERSION RATE
17.2%

MINUTES PER GOAL
136

GOALS LEFT
12

GOALS RIGHT
1

HAT TRICKS
0

HEADED GOALS
13

SHOTS
151

MAJOR CLUB HONOURS
⚽ Frauen-Bundesliga: 2013, 2014, 2017, 2018, 2019, 2020, 2022 ⚽ UEFA Women's Champions League: 2009 (Duisburg), 2013*, 2014* (*VfL Wolfsburg) ⚽ DFB-Pokal Frauen: 2009*, 2010* (*Duisburg), 2013, 2015-2023

INTERNATIONAL HONOURS
⚽ Olympics Games: 2016
⚽ UEFA Women's Championship: runner-up 2022

ACTIVITY AREAS

FRIDOLINA ROLFÖ

The left-sided forward makes speedy runs out wide and has the awareness of when to cross into the penalty area or unleash a shot. Fridolina Rolfö is an aerial presence from free-kicks and corners as she loses her marker and powers a header towards the net.

NATIONALITY
Swedish

CURRENT CLUB
Barcelona

16

DATE OF BIRTH	24/11/1993
POSITION	FORWARD
HEIGHT	1.79 M
PRO DEBUT	2008
PREFERRED FOOT	LEFT

GOALS
19

PENALTIES SCORED
4

ASSISTS
12

APPEARANCES
43

CONVERSION RATE
24.4%

MINUTES PER GOAL
167

GOALS LEFT
12

GOALS RIGHT
6

HAT TRICKS
0

HEADED GOALS
1

SHOTS
78

MAJOR CLUB HONOURS
⚽ Liga F: 2022, 2023, 2024
⚽ UEFA Women's Champions League: 2023, 2024
⚽ Frauen Bundesliga: 2020 (VfL Wolfsburg)
⚽ Copa de la Reina: 2022, 2024

INTERNATIONAL HONOURS
⚽ Olympic Games: runner-up 2016, 2020 (2021)
⚽ FIFA Women's World Cup: third-place 2019, 2023

ACTIVITY AREAS

23

NATIONALITY
English

CURRENT CLUB
Arsenal

ALESSIA RUSSO

Alessia Russo's first role is to score goals, but her skill and vision make her much more than just a striking target. She can operate in deeper areas to gain possession and then spray the ball effectively. Watch out for her clever flicks, twists and spins that outfox defenders and beat goalkeepers.

DATE OF BIRTH	08/02/1999
POSITION	STRIKER
HEIGHT	1.73 M
PRO DEBUT	2016
PREFERRED FOOT	RIGHT

GOALS
22

PENALTIES SCORED
1

APPEARANCES
42

ASSISTS
5

CONVERSION RATE
14.6%

MINUTES PER GOAL
150

GOALS LEFT
2

GOALS RIGHT
16

HAT TRICKS
1

HEADED GOALS
4

SHOTS
151

MAJOR CLUB HONOURS
⚽ FA Women's League Cup: 2024

INTERNATIONAL HONOURS
⚽ UEFA Women's Championship: 2022
⚽ UEFA Women's Finalissima: 2023
⚽ FIFA Women's World Cup: runner-up 2023

ACTIVITY AREAS

LEA SCHÜLLER

Lea Schüller enjoys the responsibility of being a top striker using her strength and expert hold-up skills to build forward momentum. Schüller's smart movement helps her find pockets of space in the opposition box, ready to time leaps over defenders and connect with a header.

NATIONALITY
German

CURRENT CLUB
Bayern Munich

DATE OF BIRTH	12/11/1997
POSITION	FORWARD
HEIGHT	1.73 M
PRO DEBUT	2013
PREFERRED FOOT	RIGHT

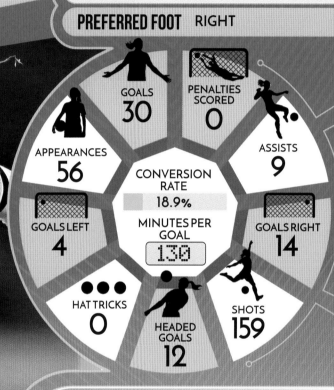

GOALS **30**

PENALTIES SCORED **0**

ASSISTS **9**

APPEARANCES **56**

CONVERSION RATE **18.9%**

GOALS LEFT **4**

MINUTES PER GOAL **130**

GOALS RIGHT **14**

HAT TRICKS **0**

HEADED GOALS **12**

SHOTS **159**

MAJOR CLUB HONOURS
⚽ Frauen-Bundesliga: 2021, 2023, 2024

INTERNATIONAL HONOURS
⚽ UEFA Women's Championship: runner-up 2022

ACTIVITY AREAS

11

NATIONALITY
American

CURRENT CLUB
San Diego Wave

JAEDYN SHAW

With seven goals in her first 12 games for the USA, the young Jaedyn Shaw is already excelling at elite level. Versatile, athletic and creative, Shaw is a big team player who can quickly assesses her options in the final third. She is hard to defend against, especially when she has an eye for goal.

DATE OF BIRTH	20/11/2004
POSITION	FORWARD
HEIGHT	1.67 M
PRO DEBUT	2022
PREFERRED FOOT	RIGHT

GOALS
11

PENALTIES SCORED
1

APPEARANCES
39

ASSISTS
4

CONVERSION RATE
16.2%

GOALS LEFT
3

MINUTES PER GOAL
227

GOALS RIGHT
6

HAT TRICKS
0

HEADED GOALS
2

SHOTS
68

MAJOR CLUB HONOURS
⚽ NWSL Shield: 2023

INTERNATIONAL HONOURS
⚽ CONCACAF Women's Gold Cup: 2024

ACTIVITY AREAS

KHADIJA SHAW

In 2024, Khadija Shaw netted her 68th goal in just 82 games for Manchester City to become the club's record scorer. Her speed and strength make her a menace in and around the box, and her power is difficult to contain, plus Shaw needs just a glimpse of the target to fire a shot away.

NATIONALITY
Jamaican

CURRENT CLUB
Manchester City

21

DATE OF BIRTH	31/01/1997
POSITION	STRIKER
HEIGHT	1.80 M
PRO DEBUT	2018
PREFERRED FOOT	RIGHT

GOALS
41

PENALTIES SCORED
1

ASSISTS
10

APPEARANCES
40

CONVERSION RATE
20.3%

MINUTES PER GOAL
80

GOALS LEFT
8

GOALS RIGHT
16

HAT TRICKS
4

HEADED GOALS
17

SHOTS
202

MAJOR CLUB HONOURS
⚽ Women's League Cup: 2022
⚽ Women's FA Cup: runner-up 2022

INTERNATIONAL HONOURS
⚽ CONCACAF Women's Championship: third place 2018, 2022

ACTIVITY AREAS

9

NATIONALITY
American

CURRENT CLUB
Portland Thorns

SOPHIA SMITH

Already a recipient of a MVP (Most Valuable Player) prize from the NWSL, Sophia Smith is an elite scorer who keeps on getting better. She keeps the ball under tight control with her dazzling right foot, has the explosive pace to get into prime positions and the shooting power and precision to test the goalkeeper.

DATE OF BIRTH	10/08/2000
POSITION	FORWARD
HEIGHT	1.68 M
PRO DEBUT	2020
PREFERRED FOOT	RIGHT

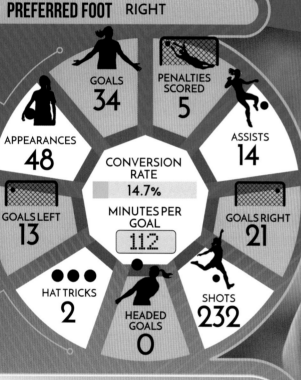

GOALS
34

PENALTIES SCORED
5

APPEARANCES
48

ASSISTS
14

CONVERSION RATE
14.7%

MINUTES PER GOAL
112

GOALS LEFT
13

GOALS RIGHT
21

HAT TRICKS
2

HEADED GOALS
0

SHOTS
232

MAJOR CLUB HONOURS
⚽ NWSL Championship: 2022
⚽ NWSL Challenge Cup: 2021

INTERNATIONAL HONOURS
⚽ CONCACAF Women's Championship: 2022
⚽ CONCACAF Women's Gold Cup: 2024

ACTIVITY AREAS

HANNAH WILKINSON

Hannah Wilkinson has bagged more than 30 goals for New Zealand in a stellar career where her work-rate and leadership has made her a fearsome striker. Wilkinson's height and heading ability gives her team a brilliant outlet, while her efforts outside the box is matched by her sharpness inside.

NATIONALITY
Australian

CURRENT CLUB
Melbourne City

17

DATE OF BIRTH	28/05/1992
POSITION	STRIKER
HEIGHT	1.76 M
PRO DEBUT	2017
PREFERRED FOOT	RIGHT

GOALS
16

PENALTIES SCORED
0

ASSISTS
3

APPEARANCES
37

CONVERSION RATE
16.8%

MINUTES PER GOAL
192

GOALS LEFT
5

GOALS RIGHT
7

HAT TRICKS
0

HEADED GOALS
4

SHOTS
95

MAJOR CLUB HONOURS
⚽ None to date

INTERNATIONAL HONOURS
⚽ None to date

ACTIVITY AREAS

GOALKEEPERS

While goal scorers win games, goalkeepers also play a huge part in helping their team to protect a victory. As the last line of defence, their acrobatics and reflexes when faced with a goal-bound shot can be the difference between winning and losing. A successful keeper uses all of her powers to command her penalty area and alongside agile and brave saves, she needs to have a strong kicking and throwing technique. No other position on the pitch has the demands or the pressure faced by the goalkeeper.

WHAT DO THE STATS MEAN?

CATCHES
This is the number of times the keeper has dealt with an attack—usually a cross—by catching the ball.

CLEAN SHEETS
Any occasion on which the goalie has not let in a goal for the full duration of the game counts as a clean sheet.

GOALS CONCEDED
This is the number of goals the keeper has conceded across two seasons in top-division football.

PENALTIES FACED/SAVED
This is the number of times a goalie has faced a penalty (excludes shootouts) and how successful she has been at saving it.

PUNCHES
This is a measure of how often the keeper has dealt with a dangerous ball (usually a cross) by punching it clear.

SAVES
This shows how many times the goalkeeper has stopped a shot or header that was on target.

Did you
know?

A penalty shootout – when each team takes penalties at the end of extra-time – is a dramatic event. A goalkeeper has the chance to be a hero by saving them and even, if needed, scoring a penalty herself.

1

NATIONALITY
Australian

CURRENT CLUB
West Ham

MACKENZIE ARNOLD

The four clean sheets Mackenzie Arnold kept at the 2023 World Cup shows just how well she performs in high-stakes games. A confident catcher and puncher, she backs herself to save penalties too — she stopped three during Australia's World Cup semi-final win over France.

DATE OF BIRTH	25/02/1994
POSITION	GOALKEEPER
HEIGHT	1.81 M
PRO DEBUT	2011
PREFERRED FOOT	RIGHT

GOALS CONCEDED
75

APPEARANCES
39

PENALTIES SAVED
3

CLEAN SHEETS
7

SAVES
147

PENALTIES FACED
5

CATCHES
35

PUNCHES
35

MAJOR CLUB HONOURS
⚽ A-League Premiership: 2014 (Perth Glory), 2018 (Brisbane Roar)

INTERNATIONAL HONOURS
⚽ FIFA Women's World Cup: fourth-place 2023

ACTIVITY AREAS

ANN-KATRIN BERGER

The tall Ann-Katrin Berger commands her area superbly and communicates very effectively with her defence. Along with a powerful goal-kicking abilities, one of her notable strengths is her concentration, pulling out quick-fire saves when she's suddenly faced with a snap shot.

NATIONALITY
German

CURRENT CLUB
NJ/NY Gotham

30

DATE OF BIRTH	09/10/1990
POSITION	GOALKEEPER
HEIGHT	1.80 M
PRO DEBUT	2009
PREFERRED FOOT	RIGHT

GOALS CONCEDED
28

APPEARANCES
35

PENALTIES SAVED
0

SAVES
92

CLEAN SHEETS
16

PENALTIES FACED
3

PUNCHES
18

CATCHES
34

MAJOR CLUB HONOURS
⚽ Women's Super League: 2020, 2021, 2022, 2023, 2024 (all Chelsea) ⚽ UEFA Women's Champions League: Runner-up 2021 (Chelsea) ⚽ Women's FA Cup: 2021, 2022, 2023 (all Chelsea) ⚽ Frauen-Bundesliga: 2012

INTERNATIONAL HONOURS
⚽ UEFA Women's Championship: runner-up 2022

ACTIVITY AREAS

1

NATIONALITY
American

CURRENT CLUB
Houston Dash

JANE CAMPBELL

An extremely consistent stopper, Jane Campbell was NWSL Goalkeeper of the Year in 2023. She is always alert in the box and is decisive when venturing forward to sweep danger away. She is confident dealing with crosses too, rising above her opponents to collect the ball.

DATE OF BIRTH	17/02/1995
POSITION	GOALKEEPER
HEIGHT	1.75 M
PRO DEBUT	2017
PREFERRED FOOT	RIGHT

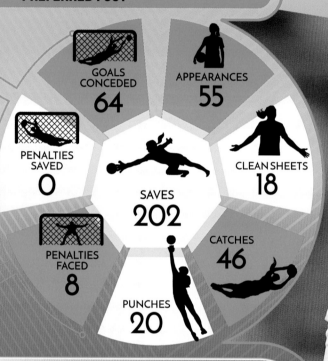

GOALS CONCEDED
64

APPEARANCES
55

PENALTIES SAVED
0

CLEAN SHEETS
18

SAVES
202

PENALTIES FACED
8

CATCHES
46

PUNCHES
20

MAJOR CLUB HONOURS
⚽ NWSL Challenge Cup: 2020

INTERNATIONAL HONOURS
⚽ CONCACAF Women's Gold Cup: 2024
⚽ Olympics: third-place 2020 (2021)

ACTIVITY AREAS

CATALINA COLL

Catalina Coll made her Spain debut during the 2023 World Cup. Her talent and razor-sharp reflexes were on show from the round of 16 onwards and she kept her place all the way to the final. Her style is to play out from the back and make perfect passes to beat the opponent's press and put her team on the attack.

NATIONALITY
Spanish

CURRENT CLUB
Barcelona

13

DATE OF BIRTH	23/04/2001
POSITION	GOALKEEPER
HEIGHT	1.70 M
PRO DEBUT	2015
PREFERRED FOOT	RIGHT

GOALS CONCEDED
6

APPEARANCES
25

PENALTIES SAVED
0

SAVES
24

CLEAN SHEETS
18

PENALTIES FACED
1

PUNCHES
4

CATCHES
4

MAJOR CLUB HONOURS
⚽ Liga F: 2021, 2022, 2023, 2024
⚽ UEFA Women's Champions League: 2021, 2023, 2024
⚽ Copa de la Reina: 2021, 2022

INTERNATIONAL HONOURS
⚽ FIFA Women's World Cup: 2023
⚽ UEFA Women's Nations League: 2024

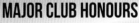
ACTIVITY AREAS

27

NATIONALITY
English

CURRENT CLUB
TBC

MARY EARPS

The technically brilliant Mary Earps makes difficult saves look easy. She catches and punches well too and transmits that confidence to her back four. The first goalkeeper to reach 50 clean sheets in the WSL, Earps has also been England's number one keeper since 2021.

DATE OF BIRTH	07/03/1993
POSITION	GOALKEEPER
HEIGHT	1.73 M
PRO DEBUT	2009
PREFERRED FOOT	RIGHT

GOALS CONCEDED
44

APPEARANCES
44

PENALTIES SAVED
0

SAVES
106

CLEAN SHEETS
21

PENALTIES FACED
2

PUNCHES
24

CATCHES
17

MAJOR CLUB HONOURS
- Women's FA Cup: 2024 (Manchester Utd)
- Frauen-Bundesliga: 2019 (VfL Wolfsburg)
- DFB-Pokal Frauen: 2019 (VfL Wolfsburg)

INTERNATIONAL HONOURS
- UEFA Women's Championship: 2022
- FIFA Women's World Cup: runner-up 2023
- Women's Finalissima: 2023

ACTIVITY AREAS

CHRISTIANE ENDLER

Acrobatic leaps for high balls and quick reflexes to block low shots make Christiane Endler super difficult to beat. Her tall, athletic frame gives her a huge advantage in one-on-one situations, where her world class reputation is most evident.

NATIONALITY
Chilean

CURRENT CLUB
Lyon

DATE OF BIRTH	23/07/1991
POSITION	GOALKEEPER
HEIGHT	1.82 M
PRO DEBUT	2008
PREFERRED FOOT	LEFT

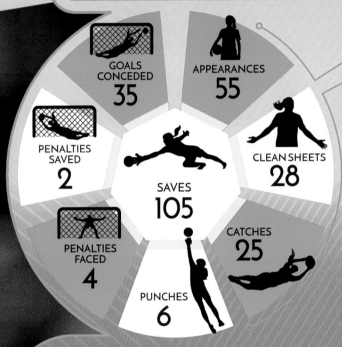

GOALS CONCEDED
35

APPEARANCES
55

PENALTIES SAVED
2

CLEAN SHEETS
28

SAVES
105

PENALTIES FACED
4

CATCHES
25

PUNCHES
6

MAJOR CLUB HONOURS
- Division 1 Féminine: 2021 (PSG), 2022, 2023, 2024
- UEFA Women's Champions League: 2022, runner-up 2024
- Coupe de France Féminine: 2018 (PSG), 2023

INTERNATIONAL HONOURS
- Copa América Femenina runner-up: 2018
- Pan American Games Silver Medal: 2023

ACTIVITY AREAS

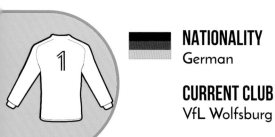

NATIONALITY
German

CURRENT CLUB
VfL Wolfsburg

MERLE FROHMS

Relishing the battle to keep her place for club and country, Merle Frohms never lets her performances drop. Aggressive but composed with her handling skills and able to pass like a cultured midfielder, she is the complete package between the posts.

DATE OF BIRTH	28/01/1995
POSITION	GOALKEEPER
HEIGHT	1.75 M
PRO DEBUT	2012
PREFERRED FOOT	RIGHT

GOALS CONCEDED
44

APPEARANCES
51

PENALTIES SAVED
0

CLEAN SHEETS
23

SAVES
104

CATCHES
9

PENALTIES FACED
4

PUNCHES
21

MAJOR CLUB HONOURS
⚽ Frauen-Bundesliga: 2013, 2014, 2017, 2018
⚽ UEFA Women's Champions League: 2013, 2014
⚽ DFB-Pokal Frauen: 2013, 2015, 2016, 2017, 2018

INTERNATIONAL HONOURS
⚽ UEFA Women's Championship: runner-up 2022

ACTIVITY AREAS

MARIA LUISA GROHS

A first-class shot stopper with the positional intelligence to match, Maria Luisa Grohs is destined to be a goalkeeping hero for many seasons to come. She works hard to improve year on year, in particular when it comes to her fitness, kicking ability and bravery on the pitch.

NATIONALITY
German

CURRENT CLUB
Bayern Munich

DATE OF BIRTH	13/06/2001
POSITION	GOALKEEPER
HEIGHT	1.80 M
PRO DEBUT	2019
PREFERRED FOOT	RIGHT

GOALS CONCEDED
32

APPEARANCES
56

PENALTIES SAVED
2

SAVES
114

CLEAN SHEETS
33

PENALTIES FACED
4

PUNCHES
12

CATCHES
33

MAJOR CLUB HONOURS
⚽ Frauen-Bundesliga: 2021, 2023, 2024

INTERNATIONAL HONOURS
⚽ None to date

ACTIVITY AREAS

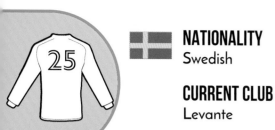

25

NATIONALITY
Swedish

CURRENT CLUB
Levante

EMMA HOLMGREN

Emma Holmgren has been flying since joining Levante in 2023. Integral to the side's patient build-up play, if her defence is sprung, she can pull out impressive saves and blocks. She is mentally strong and marshalls the back line with sureness.

DATE OF BIRTH	13/05/1997
POSITION	GOALKEEPER
HEIGHT	1.71 M
PRO DEBUT	2011
PREFERRED FOOT	RIGHT

GOALS CONCEDED
8

APPEARANCES
17

PENALTIES SAVED
0

SAVES
48

CLEAN SHEETS
9

PENALTIES FACED
0

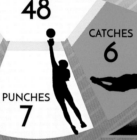
CATCHES
6

PUNCHES
7

MAJOR CLUB HONOURS
- Division 1 Féminine: 2022, 2023 (Lyon)
- UEFA Women's Champions League: 2022
- Coupe de France Féminine: 2023 (Lyon)

INTERNATIONAL HONOURS
- None to date

ACTIVITY AREAS

KHIARA KEATING

Most managers are reluctant to draft even the most talented keepers into their first team until the player is in their twenties. Khiara Keating, though, stormed the 2023/24 season aged only 19. A powerful kicker, great at closing angles and brave in blocks and saves, she is set to be a big star.

NATIONALITY
English

CURRENT CLUB
Manchester City

35

DATE OF BIRTH	27/06/2004
POSITION	GOALKEEPER
HEIGHT	1.67 M
PRO DEBUT	2020
PREFERRED FOOT	RIGHT

GOALS CONCEDED
20

APPEARANCES
25

PENALTIES SAVED
1

SAVES
67

CLEAN SHEETS
9

PENALTIES FACED
2

CATCHES
15

PUNCHES
4

MAJOR CLUB HONOURS
⚽ Women's FA League Cup: 2022

INTERNATIONAL HONOURS
⚽ None to date

ACTIVITY AREAS

1

NATIONALITY
American

CURRENT CLUB
North Carolina Courage

CASEY MURPHY

Casey Murphy has already made her mark on the world stage, registering a formidable 14 clean sheets in her first 18 senior international games. A tall keeper, she has the reach and wrists to palm away shots and towers over opponents when collecting crosses.

DATE OF BIRTH	25/04/1996
POSITION	GOALKEEPER
HEIGHT	1.85 M
PRO DEBUT	2018
PREFERRED FOOT	RIGHT

GOALS CONCEDED
63

APPEARANCES
50

PENALTIES SAVED
0

SAVES
137

CLEAN SHEETS
19

PENALTIES FACED
5

CATCHES
28

PUNCHES
24

MAJOR CLUB HONOURS
⚽ NWSL Challenge Cup: 2022, 2023

INTERNATIONAL HONOURS
⚽ CONCACAF Women's Championship: 2022
⚽ CONCACAF W Gold Cup: 2024

ACTIVITY AREAS

ZEĆIRA MUŠOVIĆ

Zećira Mušović is fast growing into a top keeper at Chelsea, who has to battle for the role with the side's other elite level stoppers. She is a super shot stopper, able to leap to the top corners and stretch low to push shots wide. She is known for her quick and accurate distribution, too.

NATIONALITY
Swedish

CURRENT CLUB
Chelsea

DATE OF BIRTH	26/05/1996
POSITION	GOALKEEPER
HEIGHT	1.80 M
PRO DEBUT	2011
PREFERRED FOOT	RIGHT

GOALS CONCEDED
11

APPEARANCES
21

PENALTIES SAVED
0

SAVES
51

CLEAN SHEETS
12

PENALTIES FACED
3

CATCHES
11

PUNCHES
5

MAJOR CLUB HONOURS
⚽ Women's Super League: 2021, 2022, 2023, 2024
⚽ Women's FA Cup: 2022, 2023
⚽ Damallsvenskan: 2013, 2014, 2015 (all FC Rosengard)

INTERNATIONAL HONOURS
⚽ FIFA Women's World Cup: third-place 2019, 2023
⚽ Olympic Games: runner-up 2020 (2021)

ACTIVITY AREAS

1

NATIONALITY
American

CURRENT CLUB
Chicago Red Stars

ALYSSA NAEHER

A two-time World Cup winner, Alyssa Naeher is lauded for her calm and composed presence in goal. She is a natural leader, effective at organising and gives orders as she zones in on a win. Her athleticism, saving technique and passing range are admirable.

DATE OF BIRTH	20/04/1988
POSITION	GOALKEEPER
HEIGHT	1.75 M
PRO DEBUT	2008
PREFERRED FOOT	RIGHT

GOALS CONCEDED
85

APPEARANCES
49

PENALTIES SAVED
1

CLEAN SHEETS
11

SAVES
159

PENALTIES FACED
9

CATCHES
22

PUNCHES
21

MAJOR CLUB HONOURS
⚽ None to date

INTERNATIONAL HONOURS
⚽ FIFA Women's World Cup: 2015, 2019
⚽ CONCACAF Women's Championship: 2018, 2022
⚽ CONCACAF W Gold Cup: 2024

ACTIVITY AREAS

CHIAMAKA NNADOZIE

Chiamaka Nnadozie's coaches praise her goalkeeping consistency and impact on the biggest stage. Never afraid to rush and smother the ball, or outjump opponents to make a catch, she remains Africa's premier stopper. She is an incredibly dependable player.

NATIONALITY
Nigerian

CURRENT CLUB
Paris FC

16

DATE OF BIRTH	08/12/2000
POSITION	GOALKEEPER
HEIGHT	1.80 M
PRO DEBUT	2016
PREFERRED FOOT	RIGHT

GOALS CONCEDED
52

APPEARANCES
47

PENALTIES SAVED
4

SAVES
128

CLEAN SHEETS
18

PENALTIES FACED
9

PUNCHES
22

CATCHES
40

MAJOR CLUB HONOURS
⚽ Nigerian Women's Championship: 2016 (Rivers Angels)
⚽ Nigerian Women's Cup: 2016, 2017, 2018 (all Rivers Angels)

INTERNATIONAL HONOURS
⚽ African Women's Championships: 2018
⚽ African Games: 2019

ACTIVITY AREAS

NATIONALITY
Spanish

CURRENT CLUB
Barcelona

SANDRA PAÑOS

Modern goalkeepers must be assured with both their hands and feet, and Sandra Paños is a fine example. Comfortable leaving her area to link passes, she also has wonderful positioning that reduces her opponents' scoring chances. She starts many of her team's moves.

DATE OF BIRTH	04/11/1992
POSITION	GOALKEEPER
HEIGHT	1.69 M
PRO DEBUT	2010
PREFERRED FOOT	RIGHT

GOALS CONCEDED
26

APPEARANCES
45

PENALTIES SAVED
2

CLEAN SHEETS
26

SAVES
64

PENALTIES FACED
3

CATCHES
21

PUNCHES
7

MAJOR CLUB HONOURS
- ⚽ Primera División: 2020, 2021, 2022, 2023, 2024
- ⚽ UEFA Women's Champions League: 2021, 2023, 2024
- ⚽ Copa de la Reina: 2017, 2018, 2020, 2021, 2022, 2024

INTERNATIONAL HONOURS
- ⚽ None to date

ACTIVITY AREAS

KAILEN SHERIDAN

Among Canada's best-ever sweeper-keepers, Kailen Sheridan is always aware of the play in front of her, ready to make passes that can open up a team. She is an imposing figure at the back, stopping headers and shots, or punching the danger clear if that is the best option.

NATIONALITY
Canadian

CURRENT CLUB
San Diego Wave

DATE OF BIRTH	16/07/1995
POSITION	GOALKEEPER
HEIGHT	1.77 M
PRO DEBUT	2013
PREFERRED FOOT	RIGHT

GOALS CONCEDED
48

APPEARANCES
50

PENALTIES SAVED
3

SAVES
160

CLEAN SHEETS
21

PENALTIES FACED
9

PUNCHES
20

CATCHES
44

MAJOR CLUB HONOURS
⚽ NWSL Shield: 2023

INTERNATIONAL HONOURS
⚽ Olympic Games: 2020 (2021)

ACTIVITY AREAS

1

NATIONALITY
Australian

CURRENT CLUB
Melbourne Victory

LYDIA WILLIAMS

Despite passing the 100 cap mark at international level, and a stellar career in the world's top leagues, Lydia Williams still wants to perform and win. She has safe hands when dealing with aerial threats and is good at anticipating shots, giving her a split second to react first.

DATE OF BIRTH	13/05/1988
POSITION	GOALKEEPER
HEIGHT	1.75 M
PRO DEBUT	2008
PREFERRED FOOT	RIGHT

GOALS CONCEDED
35

APPEARANCES
19

PENALTIES SAVED
0

CLEAN SHEETS
4

SAVES
52

PENALTIES FACED
1

CATCHES
7

PUNCHES
12

MAJOR CLUB HONOURS
⚽ A-League Championship: 2012 (Canberra United FC), 2020 (Melbourne City) ⚽ A-League Premiership: 2012, 2014 (all Canberra United FC), 2020 (Melbourne City)

INTERNATIONAL HONOURS
⚽ Women's Asian Cup: 2010

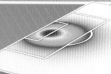

ACTIVITY AREAS

MANUELA ZINSBERGER

NATIONALITY
Austrian

CURRENT CLUB
Arsenal

With her strong saves and acrobatic ability, Manuella Zinsberger poses a challenge to the world's best opposition attacks. She suits passing-based tactics because she is confident pinging the ball to a full-back or midfielder.

DATE OF BIRTH	19/10/1995
POSITION	GOALKEEPER
HEIGHT	1.77 M
PRO DEBUT	2010
PREFERRED FOOT	RIGHT

GOALS CONCEDED
39

APPEARANCES
45

PENALTIES SAVED
0

CLEAN SHEETS
17

SAVES
94

PENALTIES FACED
2

CATCHES
31

PUNCHES
7

MAJOR CLUB HONOURS
- Frauen Bundesliga: 2015, 2016 (all Bayern Munich)
- DFB-Pokal Frauen: runner-up 2018 (Bayern Munich)
- Women's FA League Cup: 2023, 2024

INTERNATIONAL HONOURS
- None to date

ACTIVITY AREAS

MANAGERS

Managers can't score or make a save, but their work and decisions are vital to how their team plays. Also known as the head coach, they pick the players for each game and decide tactics and substitutions. They train their squad, help buy and sell players and speak to the media. The manager is the figurehead for their club. All managers are different, though. Some were great players, others had little success on the pitch before taking charge from the touchline. Take a look at the 12 in this section, the trophies they have picked up and what puts them among the top coaches in women's football.

WHAT DO THE STATS MEAN?

GAMES MANAGED
This is the number of matches the manager has been in charge of during the 2022/23 and 2023/24 seasons in top-flight football. For managers who operate (or operated) in the NWSL, the data relates to the 2022 and 2023 seasons.

TEAMS MANAGED
The figure refers to number of clubs (first teams only) that the coach has managed during their career to date.

WINS, DRAWS, LOSSES
This is the number of games the coach has won, drawn or lost during the two-season period, and includes one leg of a cup-tie, even if the tie was lost on aggregate or penalties.

TITLES AND TROPHIES
The three fields feature the manager's successes during the two-season period in the league, national and league cups and intercontinental club competitions.

JUAN CARLOS AMORÓS

NATIONALITY
Spanish

CURRENT CLUB
NY/NJ Gotham FC

Juan Carlos Amorós is extremely effective in improving players in his squad and turning a club's fortunes around. He demands an organised set-up but with attacking opportunities that can be sprung the moment his team takes possession. Juan Carlos Amorós was the 2023 NWSL Coach of the Year.

YEARS AS HEAD COACH: 13

FIRST CLUB: TOTTENHAM WOMEN

CLUBS MANAGED	GAMES	LEAGUE TITLES
4	40	1

WINS	DRAW	LOSSES
18	10	12

CHAMPIONS LEAGUE TROPHIES	OTHER TROPHIES
0	0

*Excludes Super Cups

MAJOR HONOURS (CAREER)
- ⚽ NWSL Championship: 2023

SONIA BOMPASTOR

NATIONALITY
French

CURRENT CLUB
Chelsea

After eight years coaching Lyon's academy, Bompastor took charge of the first team with instant success. In 2022, she became the first to win the Women's Champions League as player and coach. The opposition can struggle to contain her team's flexibility between a 4-3-3 and 4-2-3-1 system. Bompastor joined Chelsea in 2024.

YEARS AS HEAD COACH: 3

FIRST CLUB: LYON

CLUBS MANAGED	GAMES	LEAGUE TITLES
2	65	2

WINS	DRAW	LOSSES
54	6	5

CHAMPIONS LEAGUE TROPHIES	OTHER TROPHIES
0	3

*Excludes Super Cups

MAJOR HONOURS (CAREER)
- ⚽ UEFA Women's Champions League: 2022, runner-up 2024 (all Lyon)
- ⚽ Division 1 Féminine: 2022, 2023, 2024 (all Lyon)
- ⚽ Coupe de France Féminine: 2023 (Lyon)
- ⚽ Trophée des Championnes: 2022, 2023 (all Lyon)

JONAS EIDEVALL

Jonas Eidevall is a passionate character on the touchline. He is a highly technical coach who has Arsenal playing out from the back and looking to beat the press when not having the ball. He wants his wide forwards to torment full-backs and link with a powerful central striker around the box.

NATIONALITY
Swedish

CURRENT CLUB
Arsenal

YEARS AS HEAD COACH:	15
FIRST CLUB:	LUNDS BK

CLUBS MANAGED	GAMES	LEAGUE TITLES
3	54	0

WINS	DRAW	LOSSES
36	6	12

CHAMPIONS LEAGUE TROPHIES	OTHER TROPHIES
0	2

*Excludes Super Cups

MAJOR HONOURS (CAREER)
- ⚽ Damallsvenskan: 2013, 2014, 2019 (FC Rosengard)
- ⚽ Women's FA League Cup: 2023, 2024

JONATAN GIRÁLDEZ

Thanks to Giráldez's attractive style of play, Barcelona have been all-conquering in Spain and Europe. During his tenure, his gifted players dominated games with their skill and strength, making quick one- and two-touch passing in pockets of space to unlock defences. Giráldez moved to coach in the NWSL in 2024.

NATIONALITY
Spanish

CURRENT CLUB
Washington Spirit

YEARS AS HEAD COACH:	3
FIRST CLUB:	BARCELONA

CLUBS MANAGED	GAMES	LEAGUE TITLES
2	80	2

WINS	DRAW	LOSSES
73	4	3

CHAMPIONS LEAGUE TROPHIES	OTHER TROPHIES
2	3

*Excludes Super Cups

MAJOR HONOURS (CAREER)
- ⚽ UEFA Women's Champions League: 2023, 2024 (all Barcelona)
- ⚽ Liga F: 2022, 2023, 2024 (all Barcelona)
- ⚽ Copa de la Reina: 2022, 2024 (all Barcelona)
- ⚽ Supercopa de España: 2022, 2023, 2024 (all Barcelona)

LAURA HARVEY

With trophies in England and the USA, Laura Harvey focuses on small details that can make big differences during a game. Each player knows their role, in attacking and defending phases, and releasing wingers is often the route to how Laura Harvey beats teams who sit deep.

NATIONALITY
English

CURRENT CLUB
Seattle Reign FC

YEARS AS HEAD COACH: 17

FIRST CLUB: BIRMINGHAM CITY

CLUBS MANAGED	GAMES	LEAGUE TITLES
5	45	0

WINS	DRAW	LOSSES
19	8	18

CHAMPIONS LEAGUE TROPHIES	OTHER TROPHIES
0	0

*Excludes Super Cups

MAJOR HONOURS (CAREER)
- ⚽ NWSL Shield: 2014, 2015, 2022
- ⚽ Women's Super League: 2011, 2012 (Arsenal)
- ⚽ Women's Premier League: 2010 (Arsenal)
- ⚽ Women's FA Cup: 2011 (Arsenal)

EMMA HAYES

After a haul of medals at Chelsea, Hayes left club football to take over the USA team in 2024. She instils a winning mentality into her team, able to inspire on a one-to-one level and as a collective. Emma Hayes is tactically astute and prepares for every match knowing how to exploit the opponent's weaknesses.

NATIONALITY
English

CURRENT TEAM
USA Women's National Team

YEARS AS HEAD COACH: 22

FIRST CLUB: LONG ISLAND LADY RIDERS

CLUBS MANAGED	GAMES	LEAGUE TITLES
4	64	2

WINS	DRAW	LOSSES
49	7	8

CHAMPIONS LEAGUE TROPHIES	OTHER TROPHIES
0	1

*Excludes Super Cups

MAJOR HONOURS (CAREER)
- ⚽ Women's Super League: 2015, 2018, 2020, 2021, 2022, 2023, 2024 (all Chelsea)
- ⚽ FA WSL Spring Series: 2017 (Chelsea)
- ⚽ Women's FA Cup: 2015, 2018, 2021, 2022, 2023 (all Chelsea)
- ⚽ Women's FA League Cup: 2020, 2021 (Chelsea)

JEFF HOPKINS

The most successful coach in the A-League (formerly the W-League), Jeff Hopkins gets every drop of talent from his players. Blending experienced and exciting new prospects, the coach imparts great confidence in his team to beat any challenge in front of them with their well drilled and rehearsed tactics.

NATIONALITY
Wales

CURRENT CLUB
Melbourne Victory

YEARS AS HEAD COACH: 25

FIRST CLUB: GIPPSLAND FALCONS

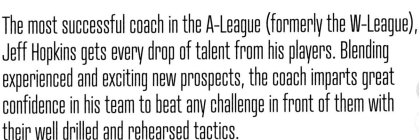

CLUBS MANAGED	GAMES	LEAGUE TITLES
4	43	0

WINS	DRAW	LOSSES
17	16	10

CHAMPIONS LEAGUE TROPHIES	OTHER TROPHIES
0	0

*Excludes Super Cups

MAJOR HONOURS (CAREER)
- ⚽ A-League: Premiers 2019
- ⚽ A-League: Champions 2021, 2022
- ⚽ A-League: Premiers 2009 (Brisbane Roar Women's)
- ⚽ A-League: Champions 2009, 2011 (Brisbane Roar Women's)

ANTE JURIC

Ante Juric's Sydney FC are extremely well set up for title challenges every year, being a strong defensive unit and possessing vision and spark in their attacks. His 4-3-3 style can convert to a back three if more numbers are needed in midfield to overpower opponents.

NATIONALITY
Australian

CURRENT CLUB
Sydney FC

YEARS AS HEAD COACH: 7

FIRST CLUB: SYDNEY FC

CLUBS MANAGED	GAMES	LEAGUE TITLES
2	46	0

WINS	DRAW	LOSSES
28	8	10

CHAMPIONS LEAGUE TROPHIES	OTHER TROPHIES
0	0

*Excludes Super Cups

MAJOR HONOURS (CAREER)
- ⚽ A-League: Premiers 2021, 2022, 2023
- ⚽ A-League: Champions 2019, 2023

CASEY STONEY

Casey Stoney followed her 2022 NWSL Coach of the Year at San Diego Wave by winning the Shield and Challenge Cup the following two years. Her team is brave in possession, creating attacking patterns that have the opposition using energy to chase and get behind the ball. Beating this manager is never easy.

NATIONALITY
English

CURRENT CLUB
Free agent

YEARS AS HEAD COACH: 15

FIRST CLUB: CHELSEA

CLUBS MANAGED	GAMES	LEAGUE TITLES
3	47	1

WINS	DRAW	LOSSES
22	10	15

CHAMPIONS LEAGUE TROPHIES	OTHER TROPHIES
0	1

MAJOR HONOURS (CAREER)
- ⚽ NWSL Shield: 2023 (San Diego Wave)
- ⚽ NWSL Challenge Cup: 2024 (San Diego Wave)
- ⚽ FA Women's Championship: 2019 (Manchester United)

*Excludes Super Cups

ALEXANDER STRAUS

Straus has dominated the German league since joining Bayern in 2023, losing just one league game in his first two seasons. His style is to take early control of a game, instructing his team to overload the midfield and create scoring chances. Bayern also work hard to take back possession quickly.

NATIONALITY
Norwegian

CURRENT CLUB
Bayern Munich

YEARS AS HEAD COACH : 11

FIRST CLUB: NEST-SOTRA

CLUBS MANAGED	GAMES	LEAGUE TITLES
3	44	2

WINS	DRAW	LOSSES
38	5	1

CHAMPIONS LEAGUE TROPHIES	OTHER TROPHIES
0	0

MAJOR HONOURS (CAREER)
- ⚽ Frauen Bundesliga: 2023, 2024
- ⚽ Toppserien: 2021, 2022 (all SK Brann)

*Excludes Super Cups

TOMMY STROOT

Tommy Stroot only turned 36 in 2024 but he already has an impressive career thanks to his skills on the training ground and matchday touchline. The German knows how to handle the demands of busy league and European schedules, having an organised 4-3-3 or 4-2-3-1 formation that creates lots of chances.

NATIONALITY
German

CURRENT CLUB
VfL Wolfsburg

YEARS AS HEAD COACH:	11
FIRST CLUB:	SV MEPPEN

CLUBS MANAGED	GAMES	LEAGUE TITLES
3	55	0

WINS	DRAW	LOSSES
42	6	7

CHAMPIONS LEAGUE TROPHIES	OTHER TROPHIES
0	2

MAJOR HONOURS (CAREER)
- ⚽ Frauen Bundesliga: 2022
- ⚽ DFB Pokal: 2022, 2023
- ⚽ Women's Eredivisie: 2019, 2021 (Twente)

*Excludes Super Cups

GARETH TAYLOR

With a strong squad at Manchester City, Gareth Taylor is not afraid to make big decisions and rest key players or use them as game-changing substitutes. A central forward who can hold the ball well, dynamic wingers and defenders who are calm when building from the back are all signs of his coaching ethos.

NATIONALITY
Welsh

CURRENT CLUB
Manchester City

YEARS AS HEAD COACH:	4
FIRST CLUB:	MANCHESTER CITY

CLUBS MANAGED	GAMES	LEAGUE TITLES
1	44	0

WINS	DRAW	LOSSES
33	3	8

CHAMPIONS LEAGUE TROPHIES	OTHER TROPHIES
0	0

MAJOR HONOURS (CAREER)
- ⚽ Women's FA Cup: 2020, runner-up 2022
- ⚽ Women's FA League Cup: 2022

*Excludes Super Cups

NOTES